MAKERS
of the
MUSLIM
WORLD

Abd al-Rahman al-Kawakibi

TITLES IN THE MAKERS OF THE MUSLIM WORLD SERIES

Series Editors: Professor Khaled El-Rouayheb, Harvard University, and Professor Sabine Schmidtke, Institute for Advanced Study, Princeton

Abd al-Ghani al-Nabulusi, Samer Akkach
'Abd al-Malik, Chase F. Robinson
Abd al-Rahman III, Maribel Fierro
Abu Nuwas, Philip Kennedy
Ahmad al-Mansur, Mercedes García-Arenal
Ahmad ibn Hanbal, Christopher Melchert
Ahmad Riza Khan Barelwi, Usha Sanyal
Akbar, André Wink
Al-Ma'mun, Michael Cooperson
Al-Mutanabbi, Margaret Larkin
Amir Khusraw, Sunil Sharma
Ashraf 'Ali Thanawi, Muhammad Qasim Zaman
Chinggis Khan, Michal Biran
El Hajj Beshir Agha, Jane Hathaway
Elijah Muhammad, Herbert Berg
Fazlallah Astarabadi and the Hurufis, Shazad Bashir
Ghazali, Eric Ormsby
Hasan al-Banna, Gudrun Krämer
Husain Ahmad Madani, Barbara Metcalf
Ibn 'Arabi, William C. Chittick
Ibn Fudi, Ahmad Dallal
Ibn Tufayl, Taneli Kukkonen
Ikhwan al-Safa, Godefroid de Callatay
Imam Shafi'i, Kecia Ali
Karim Khan Zand, John R. Perry
Mehmed Ali, Khaled Fahmy
Mu'awiya ibn abi Sufyan, R. Stephen Humphreys
Muhammad Abduh, Mark Sedgwick
Mulla Sadra, Sayeh Meisami
Nasser, Joel Gordon
Nazira Zeineddine, Miriam Cooke
Sa'di, Homa Katouzian
Shah Abbas, Sholeh Quinn
Shaykh Mufid, Tamima Bayhom-Daou
Usama ibn Munqidh, Paul M. Cobb

For current information and details of other books in the series, please visit www.oneworld-publications.com

MAKERS
of the
MUSLIM
WORLD

Abd al-Rahman al-Kawakibi

Islamic Reform and Arab Revival

ITZCHAK WEISMANN

ONEWORLD

ABD AL-RAHMAN AL-KAWAKIBI

A Oneworld Book

Published by Oneworld Publications 2015

A CIP record for this title is available
from the British Library

ISBN 978–1–78074–795–8
eISBN 978–1–78074–796–5

Typeset by Jayvee, Trivandrum, India
Printed and bound in Great Britain by Clays Ltd, St Ives plc

Oneworld Publications
10 Bloomsbury Street,
London WC1B 3SR, England

This book was published with the support of
the Israel Science Foundation.

Abd al-Rahman al-Kawakibi

For the victims of the Syrian civil war

CONTENTS

INTRODUCTION

Abd al-Rahman al-Kawakibi (1855–1902) was one of the most brilliant and articulate representatives of the first generation of modern politico-religious reformers that sprang up in the Arab provinces of the Ottoman Empire in the latter part of the nineteenth century. This group of new intellectuals helped generate the Arab renaissance (*al-nahda*) and would later become known as Modernist Salafis. Kawakibi's reputation derives from his two major published works. One is *The Nature of Tyranny and the Injuries of Enslavement* (Taba'i' al-istibdad wa-masari' al-isti'bad), a forceful diatribe against Ottoman despotism; the other is *The Mother of Cities* (Umm al-Qura, an epithet of Mecca), which is framed as a protocol of an imaginary conference held at the holy city in the pilgrimage season of 1899 to examine the reasons for the decline of Islam and suggest ways for its revival. Kawakibi's passionate defense of the merits of the Arabs in the appendix of this work earned him fame as an early precursor of Arab nationalism.

Scion of a lesser branch of a notable family of scholars and dignitaries from Aleppo in northern Syria, Kawakibi received his initial religious education within his family circle. He augmented it by acquiring vast knowledge in the modern sciences then being introduced into the city and intense reading of the Turkish newspapers arriving from Istanbul. At age twenty, he was appointed editor of the official paper of the province. Two years later, he founded the first independent newspaper in Aleppo, which published only a few issues before it was ordered to close. These marked the two seemingly contradictory paths of Kawakibi's checkered career. On the one hand, he held high posts in the expanding administration of the city under the Tanzimat reforms; on the other, he was responsible for various civil initiatives to protect the local population from arbitrary corrupt authorities. Persecuted for his free spirit and defiant action, he was twice arrested and once sentenced to death. In 1898, Kawakibi ultimately fled to Cairo where, in the four years left to him, he socialized with Syrian and Egyptian reformist colleagues, published his books and articles, and travelled widely through the Muslim world.

Kawakibi has attracted considerable attention from successive generations of Arab and Muslim writers. In numerous admiring works, he has been described as a pioneer of Arab nationalism, an enlightened Islamic reformer, and the promoter of various commendable causes such as democracy, liberalism, socialism, and secularism. Writing on Kawakibi and his teachings began early on, with the countless obituaries that appeared following his premature death in 1902. He was a constant subject of pride for the intellectuals of his hometown Aleppo, who mentioned him time and again in their books and journals. The interest in Kawakibi's legacy became particularly strong in the heyday of Arab nationalism in the 1950s and 1960s with a series of studies on his life and especially his thought. With the Islamic resurgence from the 1970s on, there was a marked shift toward the religious aspect of his legacy, often accompanied by a sharp denunciation of its secular dimension. Finally, since the 1990s, Kawakibi has been embraced as a paragon of democracy and enlightenment by Arab intellectuals opposed to oppressive Arab governments and violent Islamic radicalism alike.

In Western scholarship, by contrast, Kawakibi has often been relegated to a secondary place and paid relatively little attention. Several factors have contributed to this negligence. One is the general bias in the field of modern Middle Eastern studies toward Egypt, which overshadows other countries in the region. Egypt gained virtual autonomy from the Ottoman Empire in the course of the nineteenth century and became a leading political and cultural center under British colonial rule after the 1880s. This made it more accessible and more attractive than the Arab provinces of Western Asia, which remained under direct Ottoman control until after World War I. Indeed, like Kawakibi, many of the religious reformers and Arab activists from Lebanon and Syria escaped at the time to freer Egypt. As a result, our understanding of intellectual life in nineteenth-century Cairo advanced tremendously, while we know less about Baghdad, Damascus, or Aleppo.

Related to this is the tendency in the field of Islamic studies to focus on a line of three consecutive figures in the formation of modern Arab Islamic reform: the international revolutionary Jamal al-Din al-Afghani (1839–97), his erstwhile Modernist disciple Muhammad Abduh (1848–1905), and the latter's younger collaborator Rashid Rida (1865–1935), who in the course of World War I became a sympathizer of the Wahhabi cause and began drifting to a more purist type of Salafism. Of the three, only Abduh was Egyptian, but Afghani's career and fame were founded on his involvement in Egyptian politics and religion in the stormy decade of the 1870s, while Rida emigrated in 1897 from his native Tripoli in Syria to Egypt, where he spent the rest of his life as editor of the influential Islamic journal he had founded, *al-Manar*. Still, the substantial contribution of each of these figures to the cause of Islamic reform should not blind us to other thinkers who worked outside Egypt, nor to their interaction and mutual fertilization. At present, we have detailed biographies of Afghani and Abduh, the latter in this series of Makers of the Muslim World, but none on other, no less important, figures such as Nu'man Khayr al-Din (1836–99) and Mahmud Shukri al-Alusi of Baghdad (1857–1924), Jamal al-Din al-Qasimi of Damascus (1866–1914), or Abd al-Rahman al-Kawakibi of Aleppo.

These general considerations are further compounded by the peculiar circumstances of Kawakibi's life, which forced him to conceal much of his activity and publish anonymously. As we have seen, he eventually followed in the footsteps of his younger compatriot Rida, and many other Syrian intellectuals and journalists of the day, who escaped from the formidable censorship of the Hamidian regime and thrived in the freer atmosphere of British Egypt. Yet, though they emigrated from Syria only two years apart, Rida established himself in Cairo early in his career, while Kawakibi, who was ten years older, remained planted in his native Aleppo for much longer and decided to leave only after harassment by the authorities brought him to an impasse. But then his integration into the Egyptian intellectual scene, and his friendship with Rida and other immigrant Syrians, were cut short by his sudden death four years after his arrival.

Other common misconceptions that have obstructed full appreciation of Kawakibi's contribution to Islamic reform are related to the content and originality of his work. In two articles published in 1954 and 1955, Sylvia Haim argued that both his major books were indebted to two respective European authors who deeply influenced him. Indeed, in *The Nature of Tyranny*, Kawakibi acknowledges borrowing from Enlightenment thinkers such as the eighteenth-century Italian author Vittorio Alfieri, while *The Mother of Cities* shows some general similarity to ideas aired at the time by the English Arabophile Wilfred Scawen Blunt. Still, there is no doubt that the two books are essentially the fruit of his own spirit. Both demonstrate Kawakibi's profound acquaintance with the Islamic religious sources and methods, along with proficiency in Western political science and a keen observation of Muslim history and its current situation. The claim about his lack of originality ultimately derives from the Orientalist inclination to see all innovative ideas as coming from the modern West.

No less serious is the salient tendency in the available scholarly literature to dwell on Kawakibi's political, and especially (proto-) nationalist, ideas at the expense of his religious thought. Kawakibi's Islamic reformism was undoubtedly motivated by the political and socioeconomic realities of the late nineteenth century in general, and of his native Aleppo in particular. After all, the *nahda* was a cultural response to the Western colonial enterprise and the resulting endeavor of the Ottoman government to restructure the state along modern rationalist and capitalist lines. Such a perspective seems further justified in that late-Ottoman Syria was the cradle of Arab nationalism. It is equally evident, however, that Kawakibi's political and social thought was anchored to the Islamic living tradition of his time. As scholarly attention was drawn to Kawakibi during the heyday of Arab nationalism in the 1950s and 1960s, the religious dimension of his work was by and large lost.

A notable exception to this negligence is the only full-length monograph on Kawakibi's thought to date by the French scholar Norbert Tapiero, who tried to give a balanced view of its religious, social, and political dimensions. Albert Hourani, by contrast, dedicated only a few paragraphs to Kawakibi in his seminal work *Arabic Thought in the Liberal Age, 1798–1939*. He acknowledged that there was "something original about his writing" and expounded his major religious ideas, but chose to place the whole discussion in the chapter on Arab nationalism. Though the secularization paradigm has been largely discredited by the worldwide religious revival of the 1970s, this is hardly reflected in the few more recent scholarly studies of Kawakibi, which continue to portray him as first and foremost an Arab nationalist.

Finally, there is the problem of the sources. Kawakibi's life has been constructed on the basis of biographical sketches produced almost exclusively by family members and colleagues. The earliest were the obituaries published by Rashid Rida and other journalists in the Egyptian press in 1902, and the texts of Kawakibi's hometown friend Kamil al-Ghazzi and of his son As'ad al-Kawakibi in issues commemorating him in the Aleppine literary journal *al-Hadith* in 1929 and 1952, respectively. The first text was not only obviously overwhelmingly sympathetic, but it was also written at distance from the actual arena of most of Kawakibi's life in Aleppo, while the other two suffer from a widening gap in time, which tends to confuse dates and events. Furthermore, these early primary sources basically conformed to the traditional convention of biographical dictionaries. Following this long-established literary tradition, they dwelt, usually in an anecdotal manner, on Kawakibi's educational background, the positions he held, the principal events in his life, and his literary production, but overlooked other aspects of no less interest to the modern biographer, such as his family life, social connections, and economic standing. These deficiencies are partly set to rights by more recent biographies, most notably by his grandson Sa'd Zaghlul al-Kawakibi, who provides us with many intimate details of the family. We still lack detailed information about Kawakibi's connections with other religious intellectuals in the Ottoman Empire and Egypt, and about the history of Aleppo in the last quarter of the nineteenth century.

The result is that Abd al-Rahman al-Kawakibi's image, like the conference he convened in Mecca, *The Mother of Cities*, in 1899, has remained in some respects a mystery. This book is the first full-scale scholarly biography in English, and indeed in any

European language, of this important, though rather neglected and ill-understood precursor of modern Islamic reform and Arab nationalism. It combines a critical and contextualized examination of Kawakibi's life with a fresh look at his writings, from the newspapers he founded as a youth in Aleppo to the mature books he published in Cairo. My work takes into consideration the research carried out by Western scholars, as well as the vast Arab-Islamic literature on the man and his ideas. These are augmented by newly revealed information from family memoirs and papers, and previously untapped documents in Les archives diplomatiques du ministère des affaires étrangères in Paris and Nantes, the British National Archives in London, and Başbakanlık Osmanlı Arşivleri in Istanbul, which yielded invaluable details of Kawakibi's public life in Aleppo in the actual time and place of their occurrence and of the local circumstances in which they were played out.

The book consists of seven chapters. Chapter 1 provides the background to Kawakibi's life and thought. It discusses the political and religious landscape of late Ottoman Aleppo, the impact of his family, and his mixed traditional and modern education. Chapter 2 deals with his early journalistic enterprise, including a detailed analysis of extant issues of his two successive independent newspapers from 1878 to 1879, *al-Shahba* and *al-I'tidal*. Chapter 3 is devoted to Kawakibi's subsequent career in the Ottoman provincial administration of the Tanzimat and as a relentless opponent of corruption, and to his exile in Cairo. Chapters 4 to 6 take a fresh look at his two major works, based on the idea that their medium – a conference and a scientific investigation, respectively – is also the message. Chapter 7 concludes the book with a brief view of the fate of the Kawakibi family after his demise and an appraisal of the mixed legacy he left among Arab nationalists, Islamic reformers, and Arab-Islamic intellectuals ever since.

Abd al-Rahman al-Kawakibi and his works have fascinated me from the beginning of my academic career. It is my hope that this first comprehensive study of his career and ideas will help him gain the place he deserves in the annals of Islamic reform and the Arab renaissance of the late nineteenth century, and contribute to a better assessment of his impact on the rise of the Modernist Salafi trend at that time and on the subsequent evolution of Islamic political thought and the course of Arab nationalism during the twentieth and early twenty-first centuries.

1

THE MAKING OF A SYRIAN ISLAMIC INTELLECTUAL

POLITICS AND SOCIETY IN LATE OTTOMAN ALEPPO

Aleppo was the largest urban center in the Eastern Mediterranean throughout most of the Ottoman period, second only to Istanbul and Cairo. It served as the administrative capital of a vast province bearing its name, Halab, which extended over today's northern Syria and southeast Turkey and consisted of three districts: Aleppo, Mar'ash, and Urfa. It was also a thriving center of manufacture and a nodal point for regional as well as international trade routes ranging from Europe to the Indian subcontinent.

Aleppo's population of the eighteenth century was estimated at over 100,000 inhabitants. This measure was somewhat diminished in the first half of the nineteenth century after a devastating earthquake in 1822 and recurrent epidemics that carried off substantial parts of the population. The city began to recover after 1850 despite some new economic hardships, due mainly to delays in the construction of a carriage road to its Mediterranean port Alexandretta and the opening of the Suez Canal, which displaced the long-distance caravans that had frequented the city in the past. Yet, although overtaken by Damascus and Beirut, it continued to expand, demographically – reaching 116,000 inhabitants in 1890 – and physically – with the construction of new affluent neighborhoods to the west and northwest of the city.

As a center of long-distance commerce, Ottoman Aleppo displayed remarkable religious, ethnic, and linguistic diversity. The majority of its population were Sunni Muslims, constituting somewhere between 65 and 75 percent, but it also had a substantial Christian minority of 16 to 18 percent, most of whom, in the city as in the province at large, were Armenians of the Catholic, Greek-Orthodox, and Protestant denominations. Jews formed a smaller but still considerable community of up to 10 percent. The city was also home to a community of foreign nationals, mostly merchants from European countries, from Iran and from India. Ethnically, the urban centers of the Ottoman province of Aleppo were divided between Turks in the northern districts and Arabs in the city of Aleppo and its district. The nomad population of the Syrian Desert was predominantly Arab, while most of the rural population was of Kurdish extraction.

With the weakening of central Ottoman authority in the eighteenth century, an era of turbulence set in, affecting Aleppo's social stability and economic prosperity. From the 1760s on, two armed factions – the Janissaries, the imperial militia that increasingly relied on locals and rural migrants, and the *ashraf*, the alleged descendants of the Prophet whose number in Aleppo was particularly large – fought each other for control of the city, while Bedouin tribes exploited the opportunity to drive away the peasants from the surrounding villages and pillaged caravans. On the other hand, this period witnessed the advance of new social forces, which often allied with one another: civil Muslim families of notables (*a'yan*), which gained access to rural resources in the countryside, and minority merchants, who developed trading networks through their connections with European firms. The Kawakibi family belonged to the first group.

The Egyptian occupation of Syria in 1832 brought in its trail an unprecedented set of reforms aimed at creating strong government. Concomitantly, Christians were granted equal status, while for the first time European consulates could be set up in the major cities and missionary activity was allowed to take place in the country. In Aleppo, as in the rest of Syria, these measures met with strong resistance on the part of the Muslim leadership, whose position was undermined, and of the Muslim masses, whose religious feelings were hurt.

The restoration of Ottoman rule in Syria in 1840 heralded the inauguration of the Tanzimat reforms (1839–76), which embraced the goals of strengthening the central government and enhancing security in the provinces. Aleppo was chosen as a testing ground, and demonstrated the difficulties in effecting change in the face of a conservative Muslim society. Along with the reforms, the Anglo-Ottoman trade agreement of 1838 eventually opened Syria to Western economic exploitation through free trade. Almost nothing is recorded about the Kawakibis' standing in Aleppo at that time, which seems to indicate a certain decline in their fortunes. Of Abd al-Rahman's grandfather, Mas'ud al-Kawakibi, we know only his name.

The Tanzimat reforms intensified social and communal tensions throughout Syria. In Aleppo, the power of the paramilitary factions was undermined by the imposition of direct taxation and conscription, while the poorer sections of the Muslim population were hard hit by the inundation of the local market with cheap European goods, products of the industrial revolution. By contrast, the civil *a'yan* acquired a dominant position in the newly established local councils (sing. *majlis*), while the Christians were able to improve their standing by acting as middlemen for European interests. The ensuing uprising of 1850, which would repeat itself on a much larger scale in Damascus and other cities, was directed against the Christians, who displayed their new status through imposing churches and grand processions. Incited by the leaders of the Janissary and *ashraf* factions, the Muslim mob besieged the governor and looted the extramural affluent Christian suburbs. Dozens were killed and much property was damaged. The events provided the Ottoman government with the opportunity ultimately to eliminate militant factionalism in the city and reassert its central authority. By 1855, the year of Abd al-Rahman al-Kawakibi's birth, the Muslim notables of Aleppo and their Christian allies were firmly in place as the new "aristocracy of service" in the local and provincial administrations.

The reformist principles of the Tanzimat era were enshrined in the Imperial Edict of 1856, which under European pressure promised equality of civil and political rights to the non-Muslim subjects of the Empire. This was followed by the Land Code of 1858, which granted private title to agricultural land, and the Vilayat Law of 1864, which based the provincial administration on a balance between central control and local representation. The notable families of Aleppo, most notably the Jabiris and Mudarrisis, took advantage of the new laws to appropriate large tracts of arable land on the Euphrates and dominated the municipal and provincial councils.

The notable families supported the endeavors of the Sublime Porte to forge a new Western-inspired Ottoman identity based on the loyalty of all citizens to the territorial state. Their more reform-minded members joined the Young Ottoman opposition, which demanded representative government and fostered the love of the fatherland. In the Syrian provinces, the idea of supra-communal Ottomanism was accordingly supplemented by local patriotic feeling, which was fostered by the revival of Arab culture and disseminated through the fledgling private press. The Arab renaissance (*nahda*) was heralded by the Christians of Beirut and other Syrian cities as a counterbalance to the increasing communal strife, but it also appealed to Muslim notables, who were becoming concerned by the backward state of their society and were eager to revive and reform their faith. This reawakening enjoyed the blessing of prominent Ottoman statesmen such as Midhat Pasha, who was governor of Damascus from 1878 to 1880. One of the most ardent reformers in Aleppo was Ahmad al-Kawakibi, the father of Abd al-Rahman.

The Tanzimat culminated in the promulgation of the first Ottoman constitution and the subsequent convening of an elected parliament in 1876. But their implementation was mired in formidable obstacles, further aggravated by an economic crisis leading to bankruptcy in 1875 and military defeat by the Russians in the war of 1877–8. Thereupon, the new Sultan, Abdulhamid II (1876–1909), prorogued the parliament and established in its place his own personal autocratic rule. His regime continued and indeed accelerated the pace of reforms. Its measures in Aleppo, as recorded in its almanacs (*salname*), included pacifying the countryside, connecting the city by rail lines to Tripoli and Damascus, and introducing gas lights and streetcars in the streets. At the same time, Abdulhamid persecuted the Tanzimat statesmen and the Young Ottomans alike, and resuscitated the old political principles of Muslim supremacy and the unrestricted authority of the ruler. These were augmented by a pan-Islamic policy that emphasized his religious role as the Caliph of all Muslims. The new ideology was propagated to the masses through the popular Sufi brotherhoods, while all other opinions were silenced by draconian censorship.

The contradictions inherent in the Hamidian regime resulted in a split in the ranks of the Ottoman upper classes. In Aleppo, most senior notables, now joined by a new group of individuals promoted through the civil service, adjusted to the new social and religious conservatism of the time. A few of the lesser notables adhered to the more liberal and egalitarian aspects of the reform, while prosperous Christians and Jews began to leave for Egypt and increasingly for the West. Abd al-Rahman al-Kawakibi's career and writings indicate that he was the most fervent representative of the liberal reformist group in Aleppo.

THE URBAN RELIGIOUS LANDSCAPE

Despite its sizable population, and the rich endowments (*awqaf*) it inherited from previous epochs, Aleppo was not a major center of learning in the nineteenth century. As in other parts of late Ottoman Syria, the senior official religious posts in the city, especially those of the Hanafi mufti, who represented the dominant school of law in the Empire, and the *naqib al-ashraf*, the doyen of the Prophet's descendants, were monopolized by a few families. The highest post, that of Chief Qadi, was reserved for nominees coming from Istanbul, though its powers were gradually curtailed by the new courts of the Tanzimat. Prominent among the local religious families of Aleppo were the aforementioned Jabiris and Mudarrisis, along with the Qudsis, the Rifa'is and, in the early part of the century, the Kawakibis. The last-named family was spatially apart from the rest, being located in the mixed Jallum quarter in the southwest of Aleppo, while most other families were based in the overwhelmingly Muslim northeastern quarters of Farafira, Bayyad, and Dakhil Bab al-Nasr. Notable families of lesser status, particularly the Tirmaninis and the Hibrawis, held the position of Shafi'i mufti, the principal school of law to which the local Syrian population adhered, and supplied the city with its foremost teachers and preachers. By the mid-eighteenth century, the senior ulama of Aleppo usually went elsewhere to complete their higher education. Most went to al-Azhar University in Cairo, while others attended one of the prestigious colleges of Damascus.

The ulama families of late Ottoman Aleppo constituted part of the civil notable class that began to consolidate in the city after 1760. Their power was enhanced during the era of the Tanzimat reforms, as many of them sat on the provincial and local administrative councils. Moreover, from the 1870s, as members of the senior families throughout Syria moved to more lucrative secular positions, those of lesser families who took their place were challenged by upstart men of religion, who were favored due to their submissive service to the government rather than their piety or learning. This deterioration was particularly noticeable in the case of Aleppo, which lost control of its two major religious positions. The post of *naqib al-ashraf* was transferred in 1873 to Abu al-Huda al-Sayyadi (1850–1909), a humble Sufi claimant from a small town near Hama, who would soon be called by Sultan Abdulhamid II to Istanbul and made one of his close advisors. The post of Hanafi mufti remained in local hands for the next twenty-five years, but in 1898 was passed to another outsider from Hama, Muhammad al-Ubaysi (d. 1922), Abu al-Huda's principal protégé in Aleppo. Ubaysi won this prestigious post at the expense of a member of the Tirmanini family, whereas Abu al-Huda secured his position at the expense of the Kawakibis.

While the fortunes of the late Ottoman ulama were determined within what Albert Hourani described as the politics of notables, their evolving religious and sociopolitical worldview was expressed primarily through the idiom of Sufi reformism. Most ulama in Aleppo from the second half of the eighteenth century through the end of the nineteenth belonged to one or other of the Sufi brotherhoods that thrived in the city in this period. Like the upper ulama, the founders of these brotherhoods were usually invested outside Aleppo. The earliest was Ibrahim al-Hilali (1742–1822), founder in 1789 of the Qadiriyya-Khalwatiyya, which was connected to the rising civil notable class. During his studies at al-Azhar, Hilali merged his family

Qadiri affiliation with the reformist Khalwati way. He and his numerous disciples and followers no doubt recognized the relevance of the Khalwati endeavor to give voice to the grievances of the Egyptian common people against the tyranny of the unruly Mamluk elite to their own situation under the *ashraf*–Janissary armed factionalism in Aleppo. The Hilali lodge in the Jallum quarter, where the Kawakibis also resided, remained a rallying point for reform-minded elements in the civil notable class of Aleppo throughout the nineteenth century. Among its illustrious frequenters we find the rising merchant family of the Tabbakhs, as well as Abd al-Rahman's father Ahmad al-Kawakibi.

The Sufi reformist bent of the notable ulama of Aleppo was reinforced in the Tanzimat period by the arrival on the scene of the Khalidi branch of the Naqshbandiyya. This brotherhood was characterized by its combination of profound religious learning with active involvement in the affairs of society and firm support of the state. The first to introduce the Khalidiyya in Aleppo, Ahmad al-Hajjar (1776–1861), had followed the Qadiri-Khalwati way before moving to Damascus to become a disciple of the founder, Sheikh Khalid al-Baghdadi. Returning to Aleppo during the Egyptian occupation, he distinguished himself both as an active scholar engaged in the revival of mosques and religious schools (*madrasas*) and as intercessor with the governors on behalf of the local population. Of more consequence to the cause of reform was Hussein al-Bali (1819–55), a native of Gaza, who after his initiation into the Naqshbandiyya-Khalidiyya was invited in 1849 to Aleppo by a group of Muslim notables. In the few years he lived in the city, Bali gathered around him a group of young admirers who embraced his fervent support of the Tanzimat state reforms and his tolerant attitude toward non-Muslims. One of them was Muhammad al-Hilali, the son of the founder of the Qadiriyya-Khalwatiyya; another was again Ahmad al-Kawakibi.

After 1871, both these Sufi brotherhoods, and the reformist spirit they embodied, were challenged by the more popular Rifa'iyya, which was able to gain imperial favor through the agency of the aforementioned Abu al-Huda al-Sayyadi. Several families in Aleppo were affiliated to this brotherhood: the Rifa'is and Kayyalis, who belonged to the notable class and shared in its ascendency from the second half of the eighteenth century, and the Khayrallahs, who had recently settled in the city and established there a thriving lodge. The foremost figure in the brotherhood in Aleppo during the Tanzimat period was Baha' al-Din al-Rifa'i, who was appointed Hanafi mufti around 1865, even though, as historian Raghib al-Tabbakh points out, he lacked the knowledge required for the post. In contrast to the reformist brotherhoods, the Rifa'i appeal was generally directed to the lower and rural classes in the city and its surroundings.

After the death of Baha' al-Din in 1873, the Rifa'i brotherhood was taken over by Abu al-Huda, another newcomer who had been initiated by Sheikh Ali Khayrallah. That same year, he managed to attain the post of *naqib al-ashraf* of Aleppo at the expense of a cousin of Abd al-Rahman al-Kawakibi. He retained the post after being called to Istanbul, till the end of his life. As the Grand Sheikh of the Ottoman Empire, in 1878, Abu al-Huda laid the foundations for a magnificent *zawiya* on the eastern side of the city, handing its supervision over to his agent, Ubaysi. His father was buried as a saint in this lodge in 1894 and his own remains were transferred there in 1937. It served as a meeting place for the conservative camp and for propagating Sultan Abdulhamid's call to the masses to submit and unite behind him as Caliph. Abd al-Rahman al-Kawakibi, who had gained Abu al-Huda's enmity because of his refusal to acknowledge his claims to a sharifian pedigree, distinguished himself as a fierce opponent of this ideology.

To round out the picture, mention should be made of a fourth Sufi brotherhood that was introduced in Aleppo in the second half of the nineteenth century, the Yashruti branch of the Shadhiliyya. Propagated by a Tunisian sheikh from his main lodge in Acre, this brotherhood spread all across geographical Syria, from Aleppo in the north to Gaza in the south. It attracted members of the educated urban elites, but also disaffected groups of villagers who roamed cities and the countryside and, to the consternation of Yashruti, in his name paid heed to neither the sharia nor the state law.

Abd al-Rahman al-Kawakibi belonged to the first generation of religious intellectual reformers that sprang up in the Arab provinces of the Ottoman Empire in the latter part of the nineteenth century. These were sons of the urban religious notables who supported the late Tanzimat reforms while being influenced by the progressive ideas of the Young Ottomans. They combined in their upbringing thorough religious education of a Sufi reformist flavor with the modern sciences they acquired in the official school system established in the major centers of Syria after 1856 and a keen interest in public affairs sustained by the newspapers. In Aleppo, the group of religious intellectuals consisted of the offspring of the Sufi ulama who frequented the Qadiri-Khalwati Hilali lodge and the circle of the Naqshbandi sheikh Hussein al-Bali. Among them we find, along with Kawakibi, the above-mentioned historian Raghib al-Tabbakh (1877–1951); the writer Abd al-Hamid al-Jabiri (1864–1951); Bali's son, the city ethnographer Kamil al-Ghazzi (1852–1933); and his stepbrother, the philosopher and Arab littérateur Bashir al-Ghazzi (1857–1921), son of Bali's widow and Muhammad al-Hilali. While continuing to serve in various official positions, these intellectuals departed from the traditional framework of religious occupation and ventured into new areas such as journalism, the liberal professions, and modern education. Together they formed the close circle of friends and colleagues of Kawakibi.

The modern class of religious intellectuals that began to take shape in Aleppo, as in other cities of Syria and Iraq, in the late Ottoman period developed a new reformist idiom, which in due course would become known as Modernism-cum-Salafism. Early Modernist Salafis were very different from their contemporary conservative counterparts who dwell on the ritual purity of the ancestors and, even more so, from those calling for jihad against the entire world. Indeed, there is some commonality between these two phases of Salafism, as both call for a return to the sources of Islam – the Quran and the Prophet's example (*sunna*) – as these had been practiced by the pious forefathers (*al-salaf al-salih*). Both also share an aversion to the medieval traditions of the ulama within their schools and the Sufis within their brotherhoods, blaming them for deviations and superstitions that led to the decline of Islam. Still, unlike contemporary Salafis, their early Modernist predecessors advocated the adoption of the Western ideas of freedom, science, and rationality, and harbored a critical attitude toward the autocratic tendencies of the modernizing state. Suffocated by the Hamidian censorship and often harassed by the conservatives, some of the early reformers were muted, while others, among them Kawakibi, escaped to Egypt to air their views.

FAMILY BACKGROUND

Abd al-Rahman al-Kawakibi belonged to one of the oldest and most venerable families in Aleppo, albeit not a foremost branch of it. The Kawakibis, who were divided between Aleppo and Istanbul, boasted an illustrious lineage, which passed through Safi al-Din al-Ardabili, ancestor of the Safavid dynasty of Iran, back to Ali bin Abi Talib, the Prophet's cousin and fourth Caliph. His mother was the daughter of Mas'ud al-Naqib, mufti of Antioch, a port city, which in Ottoman times served as summer resort for Aleppo's notables. The Naqibs claimed descent from Muhammad al-Bakir, Ali's great-grandson. These alleged genealogies served to enhance the prestige of the two families as descendants of the Prophet and qualified them for the prestigious post of *naqib al-ashraf* of Aleppo and Antioch respectively.

According to the Kawakibi family tradition, their ancestor Abu Muhammad Ibrahim arrived at Aleppo from Haran, in today's ethnic Kurdish region of southeast Turkey, in the first half of the eleventh century. Another tradition maintains that the family became known as Kawakibi in the fifteenth century, after Muhammad Abu Yahya al-Ardabili settled in the city and made his living as a blacksmith of star-shaped nails (*kawakib* meaning stars in Arabic), before he became a famous Sufi. His descendants headed the family brotherhood from their mosque-lodge, *al-madrasa al-Kawakibiyya*, in the Jallum quarter. In the next century, members of the Kawakibi family were integrated into the Ottoman religious and administrative establishments and assumed high positions as muftis and qadis, as well as governors and administrators. We still find them in prominent positions in the last decades of Ottoman rule in Istanbul and Mecca, Baghdad and Aleppo. It is only with the rise of Arab nationalism in the twentieth century that such a diverse background could be deemed a disadvantage. Abd al-Rahman's grandson and contemporary biographer Sa'd Zaghlul al-Kawakibi (1924–2013) felt obliged to stress in this context that, contrary to the claims of earlier historians, the Kawakibis were not Iranian or Turkish or Kurdish, but purely Arab.

After 1760, the leaders of the family branch in Aleppo were Ahmad al-Kawakibi (d. 1783) and his son Hasan (d. 1814). Ahmad was a renowned jurist, who thrice served as mufti of the city, and in the final years of his life was its *naqib al-ashraf* as well. He accumulated considerable wealth in urban and rural property, including a large house in the northwestern Bandara quarter, a mill on the Quwayq River, and a soap factory. On top of all this, he renovated the family *madrasa* and provided it with a rich library, which included many manuscripts of his ancestors. The library was dispersed in Abd al-Rahman's time, his efforts to rescue it being to no avail. Hasan al-Kawakibi, the family head at the turn of the nineteenth century, benefited from his father's advancement; he too became *naqib al-ashraf* and mufti of Aleppo, and distinguished himself as a cultivated poet. We hear nothing of his progeny, which seems to indicate that the Kawakibis had never fully recovered from the calamities of the early nineteenth century and the Egyptian occupation.

The Kawakibis return to the historical record, though through a less eminent branch of the family, with Abd al-Rahman's father Ahmad Baha'i (1829–82), who established himself as a prominent member of the reformist *a'yan* in late Tanzimat Aleppo. Ahmad received the conventional religious education of his time with local ulama and imbibed the Sufi reformist tradition through his close ties with the long-established Hilali lodge. He was also one of the foremost disciples of the Naqshbandi scholar Hussein al-Bali. In 1856, Ahmad was appointed administrator of the family mosque, where he served as teacher, prayer leader, and preacher. In the course of his life, he also officiated in some of the highest religious posts in his city, as teacher in the Umayyad mosque, the principal mosque of Aleppo, secretary of the *fatwa* office, and, though allegedly reluctantly, qadi of Aleppo.

Still, as is often the case with intellectuals in general, and the Syrian reformers of the late nineteenth century more particularly, Ahmad al-Kawakibi's cultural capital, to use Bourdieu's terminology, did not match his economic capital. Although he owned some land and held prestigious positions, he was often short of money. Therefore, along with his more traditional occupations, he also specialized in writing legal deeds, for which purpose he mastered the Turkish language. He was thus among the first in Aleppo to capitalize on the needs of the expanding Ottoman administration of the Tanzimat, a track that would be greatly elaborated, though in different directions, by his two sons, the older Abd al-Rahman and the younger (by a second wife) Mas'ud. Ahmad also had two daughters, Fatima and Asma, about whom we typically hear nothing. As a civil notable and ardent supporter of the reforms, it was only natural that Ahmad would sit on Aleppo's provincial council in the final years of his life.

BETWEEN TRADITIONAL AND MODERN EDUCATION

Abd al-Rahman was born to Ahmad Baha'i and Afifa al-Kawakibi on the 23 of Shawwal 1271, which corresponds to 9 July 1855. There is some confusion about his year of birth, as his official biography states that he was born in 1849. The source of the confusion was Abd al-Rahman himself, who in 1876 obtained official confirmation of the older age so that he could become eligible for the first elections to the Ottoman parliament, which took place that year. This did not help him though, because some rival notables caused a commotion and managed to have his candidacy removed. Abd al-Rahman al-Kawakibi was thus born during the Crimean War, which greatly accelerated the progress of the Tanzimat reforms and exposed the extent of Ottoman dependence on the Western European powers.

Abd al-Rahman's childhood was overshadowed by the death of his mother. His father decided first to commit the four-year-old boy to the care of her sister Safiyya in Antioch. She was an exceptionally cultivated woman, and under her supervision he learned to read and write and began to speak Turkish, then as now the principal language in the city. After he was taken back to Aleppo, for the next two years Abd al-Rahman attended a Quranic school, where he memorized parts of the Holy Book and studied Arabic grammar, as well as advancing his knowledge in Turkish and acquiring the essentials of the Persian language. We don't know how significant that school was in Aleppo's educational landscape, but its choice may well have reflected Ahmad's awareness of the growing importance of these languages for building a noteworthy career in the era of the Tanzimat reforms.

Indeed, Ahmad was determined to give his son the best education, as befitted the scion of a long established notable family such as the Kawakibis. By then, a government secondary school (*rushdiye*) was operating in Aleppo, but Ahmad knew better than to place his son there. After finishing the Quranic school, Abd al-Rahman was sent to a private school in Antioch, about which we are only told that he could benefit there from prominent scholars on his mother's side, one of whom was later to be a member of the Ottoman parliament and another a private tutor of Abbas Hilmi II, the last Khedive in Egypt. A year later, at the age of eleven, Abd al-Rahman enrolled in the Kawakibi School, which his father as the head of the family administered. Ahmad took it upon himself to introduce his son to the religious and Arabic sciences, the conventional subjects taught in a *madrasa*. Among his other prominent teachers were two specialists in the Hanafi jurisprudence, namely Abd al-Qadir al-Habbal (1821–83), who was also a Sufi adept in the Qadiriyya-Khalwatiyya brotherhood, and Muhammad Ali al-Kahil (1818–87), who was to follow Ahmad as *amin al-fatwa* of Aleppo in 1876.

As a man of the Tanzimat, Ahmad al-Kawakibi was not content with this mode of traditional learning. Along with Abd al-Rahman's studies in the family *madrasa*, which were brief anyway, a private tutor imparted to him some knowledge of the modern sciences. The person his father chose for this purpose was Khurshid Effendi, a highly respected Turkish man of letters, who also helped the boy perfect his Turkish and improve his Persian. Perhaps under the influence of this teacher, he also learned Arab poetry, the mark of the cultivated man of the Arab renaissance. In the following years of adolescence, Abd al-Rahman developed a keen interest in a broad array of subjects from mathematics and the natural sciences to politics and history. He never learned any European language, but was an avid reader of the newspapers and journals that circulated in those years from Istanbul and Beirut, and included translations of scientific articles as well as political and cultural essays from the West. From them he could also learn of the constitutional and patriotic ideas of the Young Ottomans. Unlike his father, who still bore the title of sheikh, Abd al-Rahman al-Kawakibi was to be known merely as *sayyid* in reference both to his sharifian descent and his profane occupations. Nevertheless, he remained a staunch believer and a practicing Muslim all his life, and wore the *amama*, the turban distinctive of the ulama class.

A comparison of Abd al-Rahman's course of studies with that of his younger brother Mas'ud may help us better realize the constraints that beset the local education system of Aleppo in the 1860s, as well as the family's response to the new opportunities that opened up with the progress of the Ottoman reforms in the city in the 1870s and 1880s. Mas'ud al-Kawakibi (1864–1929) was nine years younger than Abd al-Rahman, and so obviously had a different mother. Like his elder brother, he studied Hanafi jurisprudence and Arabic with their father and other teachers in the Kawakibi School. But unlike Abd al-Rahman, Mas'ud enrolled in Aleppo's government secondary school, where he could study not only Turkish and the basics of modern sciences, subjects that his elder brother acquired from a private tutor, but also elementary French, which Abd al-Rahman had never learned. Mas'ud's private teachers focused on strengthening his French, a reflection of his father's recognition of the growing role of the European consuls in the imperial and provincial politics and economy. Mas'ud was interested in Arabic calligraphy rather than poetry and, perhaps also under the inspiration of the *nahda*, learned the Hebrew and other alphabets. Mas'ud followed Abd al-Rahman faithfully in his extensive self-reading in the natural and human sciences, which prepared both for the role envisaged for them by their father as notable religious intellectuals. But, as Mas'ud would also officiate as Friday preacher (*khatib*) and the city's *naqib al-ashraf*, he was referred to as sheikh.

Kawakibi was a family man. Sometime in the mid-1870s, when he was around twenty, he married Fatima, daughter of Sheikh Muhammad Ali al-Kahil, his erstwhile teacher at the Kawakibi School. She remained with him all along and bore him five sons: Kazim, As'ad, Rashid, Ahmad Nu'man, and Fadil, and four daughters: Afifa, Adawiyya, Bahiyya, and Nazira. As was customary among notable families of the time, he had a personal servant, Bidrus, and a nanny for his children, a black female slave named Hijab al-Nur, who lived with them. Kawakibi had freed her with the promise to return her to her homeland in Sudan but never had the opportunity to do so. She was still caring for his grandchildren when she died at an advanced age in Aleppo.

2

EXPERIMENTS IN JOURNALISM

OFFICIAL AND PRIVATE EDITOR

Abd al-Rahman al-Kawakibi's interest in contemporary affairs in general, and his mastery of Turkish in particular, won him his first position in the Ottoman administration, as editor and translator of the official gazette of the Aleppo province, *al-Furat* (the Euphrates). This was in October 1875, when he reached the age of twenty and had already published some articles in this paper. *Al-Furat* had been founded eight years earlier by the then *vali* of Aleppo, the noted historian Jevdet Pasha, who, like other reformist governors throughout the Syrian provinces, felt the need for a vehicle to transmit the central government's instructions and clarify the official standpoint on current events. It was a bilingual Turkish-Arabic weekly designed primarily for state officials, who were required to buy it, but as the only paper in the *vilayet* it had a much larger circulation. As editor, Kawakibi replaced Abd al-Qadir al-Qudsi, a close associate of Abu al-Huda al-Sayyadi, who was appointed secretary to the Sultan in Istanbul. He continued in this occupation for five years, until he in turn was replaced by his close friend the noted Aleppine ethnographer Kamil al-Ghazzi.

While still at *al-Furat*, Kawakibi also became editor of the first private paper in Aleppo. *Al-Shahba* (The Grey, the epithet of the city, reflecting the widespread use of grey stone in its architecture) appeared in May 1877, not without difficulties due to the reputation he had already gained for his progressive ideas. The paper was launched at the time of the convening of the first Ottoman parliament and in the setting of the disastrous Russian-Ottoman war, both arousing much interest and concern among reformist circles and the people at large across the Empire. It was at this time that Jamal al-Din al-Afghani began encouraging his disciples in Egypt to write for newspapers and fashion public opinion. In Aleppo, this was a period of utter chaos, as the corrupt and indifferent *vali* Kamil Pasha gave free rein to murder and robbery in the streets. The British consul Hendersson wrote at the time that, "the administration is in a state of complete anarchy. The heads of the different departments disputing and quarrelling as to their share of the spoils like wolves over a carcass ... each one for himself and all taking advantage of the disorganisation at the capital." Unlike Afghani and Abduh, and contrary to the claims of today's detractors of Kawakibi, there is no evidence that he ever joined the Freemasons in Aleppo.

Al-Shahba was registered under the name of an enterprising colleague of Kawakibi, variously called Hashim al-Attar, al-Kharrat, or, in the Turkish documents, Shekerji. His first application for a license had been approved in December 1875, with the proviso that the paper avoid politics and restrict itself to science and the arts. When the license for a full-fledged paper was eventually issued a year and a half later, Kawakibi bought a printing press to bring it out. Its name appears on the front page as the Aziziyya Press. *Al-Shahba* was a latecomer in the journalistic efflorescence of the Lebanese-Syrian Arab renaissance (*nahda*), appearing on the scene when the Tanzimat reform era was about to succumb to the autocratic rule of

Sultan Abdulhamid II. Predominantly a political paper, it heavily relied on the telegraph office, opened in Aleppo in 1864, which brought in news from the front and reports from other newspapers. To these Kawakibi added his comments on the war and on foreign and local affairs, often with the help of a highly informative historical background aimed at enlightening the readers.

Al-Shahba proved to be more radical than most older Syrian papers. Translating the constitutional and patriotic ideas of the Young Ottomans to the local provincial scene, Kawakibi did not hesitate to criticize head-on the governor and his lieutenants, as well as the imperial government, and to suggest far-reaching reforms. Such an independent tone was welcomed by politically conscious Aleppines, but it far exceeded what the conservative governor Kamil Pasha was ready to endure. The paper was first suspended immediately after the second issue by a decision of the provincial council of September 1877, and closed down completely after sixteen issues. Kawakibi's explanation for the suspensions of his paper was rather different, hinting at an otherwise unknown event in the history of late-Ottoman Aleppo. In an editorial written after the second renewal of *al-Shahba* and before its final closure, he argued that the government wrongly assumed that it was the mouthpiece of an association that had formed at that very time in the city, with the aim of "aiding politics by inspecting the working of the administration and by the use of literary influence to relieve the country from the ordeals caused by the transgressions of the powerful." Kawakibi claimed that he had no hand in the new association, though it is hard to believe that he would have stayed away from an initiative almost identical to his own and which many of Aleppo's educated class supported.

As with most other private papers of the period, Kawakibi was both the editor and principal writer in *al-Shahba*. He continued in these roles even after his ostensible replacement by his colleague Mikhail al-Saqqal, in an attempt to put a stop to the paper's constant harassment. Like Saqqal, the few other contributors to the paper were mostly Christians, who figured as the protagonists of the *nahda* in Aleppo. Following the example of his more experienced colleagues in the other cities of Syria, Kawakibi printed on the front page of his paper imperial decrees and official statements, which he could easily reproduce from *al-Furat*. In the absence of correspondents, he also followed the common practice of reprinting news items and opinion articles from other papers, be they Arab, Turkish, or European. These included *al-Jawa'ib* (The News) from Istanbul, the most popular Arabic paper of the time; *al-Janna* (The Garden), which was edited by Butrus al-Bustani, doyen of the Lebanese cultural awakening; and a variety of English and French newspapers. At the same time, Kawakibi's articles were reproduced or commented upon in other Arabic papers, notably *Thamarat al-Funun* (Fruits of the Sciences) of Beirut, the leading Muslim paper in Syria, which had been founded two years prior to *al-Shahba* and, thanks to its manifestly conservative and pro-Ottoman stance, lasted until 1908. Kawakibi was this paper's agent in Aleppo.

Undeterred by the closure of *al-Shahba*, in July 1879, following the arrival of the new governor Ghalib Pasha, Kawakibi renewed his journalistic initiative under a new name, *al-I'tidal* (Moderation). This weekly, which was registered under the name of another colleague, appeared at the demand of the authorities, like the official *al-Furat*, as a bilingual Turkish-Arabic paper. Its name notwithstanding, *al-I'tidal* continued in the same critical line of *al-Shahba* and ultimately met with a similar fate. Following repeated complaints sent to Istanbul, the journal was once suspended and fined, before it was forced to close after three-and-a-half months and a mere ten issues. The final closure

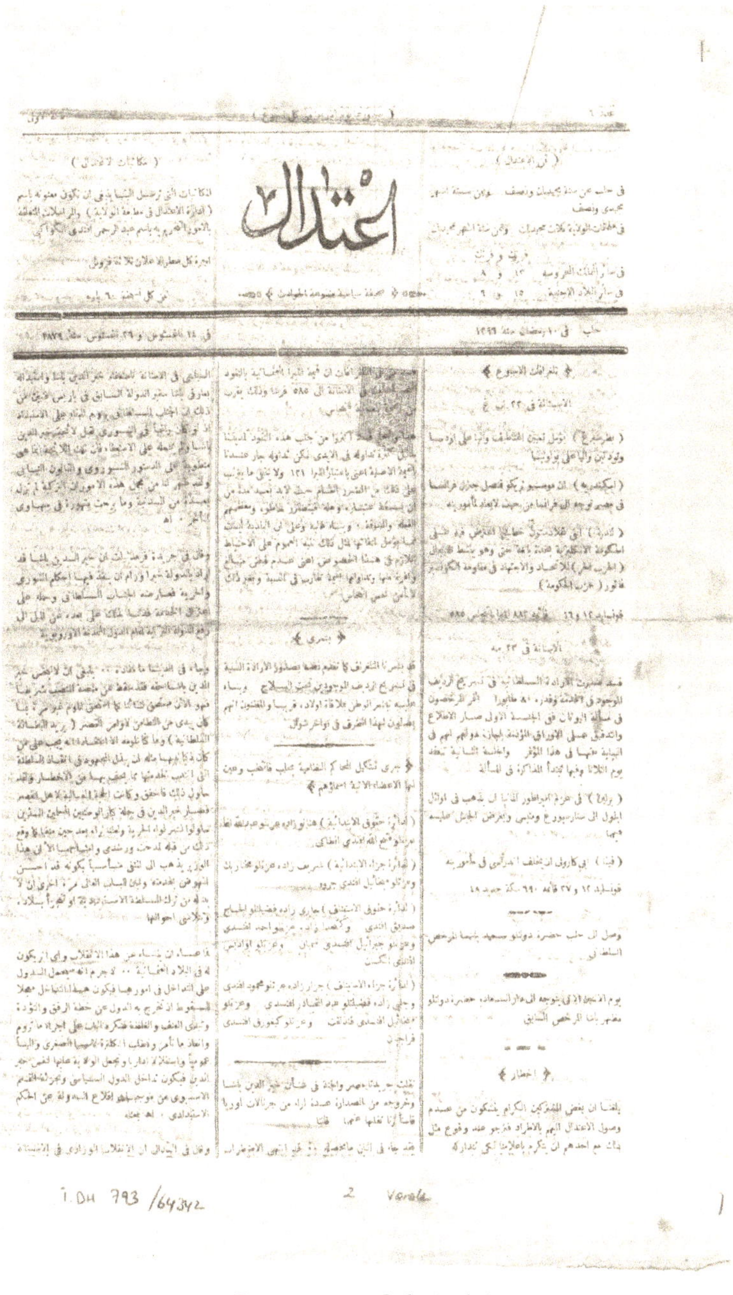

اعتدال

Front page of al-I'tidal

coincided with the news from Istanbul heralding the demobilization of the reserve army and the return home of the conscripts in the Russian-Ottoman war. The Ottoman archives have preserved requests to renew the publication of *al-I'tidal* in July 1889 and of *al-Shahba* in April 1893, but both were rejected. Kawakibi's two short-lived papers of the late 1870s thus remained the only private papers to appear in Aleppo until he left the city in 1898, although his articles continued to appear through those years, usually anonymously, in the periodicals of Cairo, Damascus and Beirut.

THE VOCATION OF THE PRESS

Abd al-Rahman al-Kawakibi's venture into the field of journalism testifies to a vivid political consciousness, as well as awareness of the role of the printed word in creating free public opinion. His courageous editorship of the official provincial gazette and of his own two private papers established him as one of the pillars of the *nahda* in Aleppo, on a par with his colleagues in the city and in the more established Arab cultural centers of Beirut and Cairo. While some of Kawakibi's ideas found their way into the pages of *al-Furat*, it was *al-Shahba* and *al-I'tidal* that reflected most faithfully his thought at this early stage of his life. More than other journalists of the *nahda*, Kawakibi insisted on speaking truth to power in them, regardless of the frequent suspensions and the substantial financial losses he incurred.

Accordingly, we now proceed to examine in more detail the extant issues of *al-Shahba* and *al-I'tidal* in order to discern the political and cultural ideas held by Kawakibi at the very beginning of his career. The analysis of his articles and commentaries will throw into relief the reformist ideas that prevailed among the intellectual circles of Aleppo in the closing years of the late

Tanzimat period in general, and shed further light on the views that a cultivated young Muslim notable such as he could acquire at home and from his teachers at that time in particular. No less importantly, these early writings will help us identify Kawakibi's sources of inspiration and provide us with the starting point for examining the evolution of his thought in the succeeding years under the rule of Sultan Abdulhamid II, and particularly for comparison with his mature works: *The Nature of Tyranny* and *The Mother of Cities*. We are largely indebted in the following analysis to Prof. Jan Daya, who was able to locate nine issues of *al-Shahba* and one issue of *al-I'tidal* in the public library of Halle in former East Germany. The following builds on his study, on another issue of *al-I'tidal* I found in the Ottoman Archives, and on articles by Kawakibi that could be retrieved from other papers.

In his inaugural editorial of *al-Shahba*, Kawakibi declares that the only motive behind the publication of the new paper is his love of the fatherland (*ghayra wataniyya*) and care for the Arab people (*hamiya Arabiyya*), and that its reports and commentaries are designed to spread knowledge, inculcate civilized manners, explain events, arouse public consciousness, assist the state in local affairs, and protect the rights of the people. He points out that the annual subscription to the paper barely covers the costs of production, and urges readers to contribute to such an important enterprise for the public good, as is the custom among the European nations. He concludes with an expression of hope to receive the support of the government of the exalted Sultan Abdulhamid. The inaugural editorial of *al-I'tidal* likewise maintains that the press is the noblest way to serve the fatherland, and deplores its repression at the hands of the former *vali*, "only because he was the enemy of freedom." Kawakibi assures the readers that the new paper is similar to the earlier one, and that it will continue to fulfill the duties incumbent on the local press:

publish important administrative measures, expose officials' blunders, present the needs of the country to the authorities, and publish scientific and political studies to educate and enlighten the people. Lastly, he asks that his attention be drawn to any error that might occur in the paper, "because newspapers are dependent on the acceptance and the good will of the public."

THE AFFLICTIONS OF THE OTTOMAN SYSTEM

Al-Shahba's close reportage of the Russian-Ottoman war and Kawakibi's analyses censuring the Russians' motives and conduct leave little doubt as to the sincerity of his loyalty to the Ottoman state. For him, as for the other leaders of the *nahda*, there was no contradiction between the principles of Ottomanism and Arabism; rather they complemented each other. This, however, did not prevent Kawakibi from spelling out in an article his harsh judgment of the conduct of the war and, in consonance with the critical ideas of the Young Ottomans, of the general corruption of the Ottoman administration, which obstructed the course of reform. The roots of the lack of success on the part of the architects of the Tanzimat went back, in his opinion, to the Ottoman Sultans' long-established practice of isolating themselves from the people. Thus, they acquired no political experience before assuming power and spent most of their time with their wives and concubines. Their tyrannical government was exercised through their servants and retinue, who showed the same traits of incompetence, love of pomp and sycophancy. The results, as Kawakibi observed them in his time, were that criminals were not punished, officials bore no responsibility for their work, politicians paid bribes to obtain meaningless ranks, and administrative posts were handed over to incompetents with no incentive to succeed. Such a system also meant that all government positions were reserved for the Turkish ruling group, to the exclusion of the Arabs. Kawakibi was careful to conclude this bold piece with the assertion that Sultan Abdulhamid II introduced many administrative measures that led to palpable improvements. This, however, did not save him from another suspension of his paper.

Contrary to what Kawakibi's biographers would later claim, his attitude to Abdulhamid at that point in time was indeed fairly positive. In 1877–8 the intentions of the new Sultan were still largely unknown, and the Tanzimat statesmen were confident that with him arbitrary government was finally over. Their hopes were propped up by the installation of the Ottoman parliament in March 1877, two months prior to the inauguration of *al-Shahba*. Kawakibi who, we may recall, had attempted to have his day of birth backdated in order to qualify for election, shared their optimism:

> There is no doubt that the formation of this council [the parliament] is among the greatest proofs that Divine providence still encompasses this Ottoman nation (*umma*). The understanding, concord and harmony that prevail among its members promises to bring us the fruits we are expecting from it. The previous tyrannical measures, from which his Highness the great lord Sultan Abdulhamid II has freed us, almost brought us to despair of correcting the situation and putting things to order. But now once again there is hope of achieving happiness.

Kawakibi's appreciation of Abdulhamid was demonstrated once again in the summer of 1879, when he expressed his confidence that, thanks to the Sultan's inclination to peace, a settlement of the borders between the Ottoman Empire and Greece was imminent.

Kawakibi was likewise optimistic about the future of the press, whose two-pronged mission in his eyes was to enlighten the public and keep watch on the government. When *al-Shahba* was first suspended for three months, Kawakibi was willing to portray it as part of the hardships typical of the beginnings of the press everywhere, in Europe in Gutenberg's time as in the Ottoman Empire and the Arab lands when it was imported there in the eighteenth and nineteenth centuries. He therefore reassured the authorities that the aim of his paper was only to benefit and glorify the state and the country.

NEW HOPES FOR ALEPPO

The same traits characterize Kawakibi's reports on the local affairs of Aleppo and his commentaries on the effect of Ottoman rule and its reforms on the city and the province. The local news section on the back page of his papers referred to public projects and important events, but without the habitual false praises of the governor and his officials that could be found in many journals of the period. One of the first issues of *al-Shahba* discussed the problem of the palpable decrease in Aleppo's population, while the first issue of *al-I'tidal* described approvingly the setting up of a provincial tax department to replace the oppressive tax farming system (*iltizam*) in the countryside. In addition, Kawakibi announced his intention to publish a series of articles on the history of the city, since, as he wrote, "love of the fatherland is among the major principles that arrange our world order, and the only means to inhabit the country, bring it success and protect its honor and rights." This intention would be realized years later in a comprehensive way by his friends and colleagues Kamil al-Ghazzi and Muhammad Raghib al-Tabbakh, whose works remain to this day an invaluable source for the study of Aleppo.

Yet even on the local level Kawakibi's patriotic feelings did not blind him to the shortcomings of the people of Aleppo in general, and to their obstinate resistance to the course of the Tanzimat reforms in particular. The roots of these evils, he maintained, lay likewise in four centuries of Ottoman misgovernment, which accustomed Aleppo's society to all kinds of harmful practices and corrupted public opinion. Faults such as the purchase of posts, meekness before superiors and bribery are extremely difficult to correct, he pointed out, since people tend to reject whatever contradicts their established beliefs and habits. What sustained them in Aleppo, perhaps more than in more advanced cities such as Beirut or Cairo, were in his view the essentially conservative position of the religious notables, whose influence remained enormous, the duplicity of the upper classes determined to cling to their privileges, and the ignorance of the common people, who continued to follow their masters blindly.

Kawakibi knew that much of the antagonism to the state derived from the high-handed manner in which the Tanzimat reforms were imposed on the inhabitants of Aleppo. He therefore saw a positive step in the recent promulgation of a new city council law, which he published in installments in three consecutive issues of *al-Shahba*, calling on his enlightened fellow citizens to shoulder the task:

> We must elect for them [the city councils] people of distinction, persons who are known for their trustworthiness, honesty and integrity, those who cherish the common good and prefer the interests of the fatherland (*al-watan*) over their personal interests. We must also beware not to restrict our elections to the notables or to certain families, but to look for those with the required attributes whoever they be, even if they are from among the common people. And we must recognize that the new ordinances delegate substantive powers to this council, so we should not neglect and scorn it as we have done in the past, when nobody wanted to be among its members except for the unworthy.

A year later, in the first issue of *al-I'tidal*, Kawakibi went out of his way to explain to the elected members of the public reforms committee, and the Aleppo public at large, what an opportunity they were being given to shape the future of their province. By his understanding, this committee was authorized to inspect the workings of the provincial administration, identify its shortcomings and specify the reasons for its malfunction, and then to suggest appropriate measures to correct and regulate the situation. These were to be incorporated into an administrative law that would guide government action in the province. Our state, Kawakibi exclaimed, has given us more than we could have hoped for. It has delegated to us the freedom to look into the affairs of our country, and we must prove our competence and accomplish the task. You members of the reforms committee, he continued, represent half a million people, who commissioned you to act on their behalf for the public good. You should thank them for the trust they have placed in you, and do your utmost to realize their hopes to improve the administration and education, develop agriculture, build roads, and reform the court system. As in the case of the Ottoman parliament, Kawakibi believed that the success of this elected body ultimately depended on cooperation and mutual support among its members.

COMMUNAL TROUBLES

The other major affliction in the social fabric of Aleppo, and in the Ottoman Empire at large, was in Kawakibi's view the deterioration in its inter-communal relations, especially Muslim–Christian relations. Indeed, the first suspension of *al-Shahba* took place after he refused to give the name of his informant about an incident in which six Armenians who wanted to volunteer for the army were rejected unless they took Muslim names. In another incident, he urged the governor to take strong action against a band of drunken Muslims who harassed priests and extorted money from Jewish passersby. Pointing to the multi-communal nature of the vast Ottoman lands, and to the difficulties of managing their different interests, Kawakibi argued that the government's traditional predilection for the Muslims embittered its Christian subjects and opened the door to intervention by foreign powers on their behalf. On the other hand, he maintained that the history of the Syrian lands showed that the Arab-Muslim conquerors had been characterized by religious tolerance, and that it was the Crusaders who introduced religious fanaticism into the country and infected Islam with its evils. He therefore concluded that neither the Ottoman government nor its Christian subjects were to be condemned, but religious fanaticism as such.

Moreover, here again Kawakibi felt there was some room for hope. In the past twenty years, he maintained, namely since the promulgation of the Imperial Edict of 1856, the government had changed course by promising equal rights to all citizens, regardless of their faith, and began incorporating Christians into the imperial administration. He was painfully aware of the commotion this policy aroused – a euphemism for the communal uprising in Aleppo in 1850 and the much bloodier massacres of Christians in Damascus and Lebanon a decade later – but he was of the opinion that it helped forge a common Ottoman identity. Its consolidation was sealed in the present war with Russia, in which "the name Ottoman became widespread and all means were used to join all subjects (*ra'iya*) in a unified national feeling (*jinsiyya*) under this name." Evidence of this development could be found in the decision of the Ottoman parliament to appoint members regardless of their communal or religious affiliation, and in the new imperial order, which had just been announced in Aleppo and was faithfully reproduced in *al-Shahba*, to the effect that members of all religious communities were to be conscripted to military service. The first suspension of the journal, therefore, was the result of Kawakibi's insistence on the implementation of this law in the face of a recalcitrant governor and Muslim population.

What were then the ideas that animated Abd al-Rahman al-Kawakibi at this early stage of his career, as these were reflected in his articles and commentaries on the pages of his papers *al-Shahba* and *al-I'tidal*? Our analysis has shown that, like the Young Ottoman movement, he was a strong supporter of reform based on three major principles: patriotism, equal citizenship, and political participation. The fatherland Kawakibi referred to ranged from his own city of Aleppo through the Syrian Arab provinces to the Ottoman Empire at large; the equality he espoused was in his eyes particularly pertinent to the Christian, as well as Jewish, communities in Syria and throughout the Ottoman domains; representative bodies with inspection powers over the government on both the local and imperial levels were for him the remedy for arbitrary and corrupt rule. One central issue was nonetheless conspicuously absent from Kawakibi's thought at this stage, at least in its journalistic expression. This was the religion of Islam.

Al-Shahba and *al-I'tidal* appeared at a particularly auspicious moment in the history of the Ottoman reform movement, when the installation of the parliament and the formation of city councils in the provinces seemed to herald a shift in the conduct of the Tanzimat statesmen from an administrative *fiat* to representative government. This moment, which also facilitated the publication of his papers, made the young Kawakibi confident that the way was now open to a rule of justice that would bring in its wake enlightenment and prosperity for the people and help fortify the state against external enemies such as Russia. It was soon to be over, however, as Sultan Abdulhamid prorogued the parliament and consolidated his personal rule for the next thirty-three years. Two of the mainstays of the new Sultan's government – strict censorship and the pan-Islamic ideology – put an end to Kawakibi's style of journalism while turning his attention to the need for religious reform.

3

A PROVINCIAL OTTOMAN NOTABLE'S CAREER

FACING THE HAMIDIAN REGIME

Kawakibi's initial experience as a journalist marked the two trajectories along which his public career would proceed in the next two decades in Aleppo. On the one hand, as a gifted son of a distinguished notable family, albeit a lesser branch of it, he advanced through a succession of official positions in the rapidly expanding local and provincial administrations, most notably in the educational, judicial, and economic fields. Many of these posts were honorary, with no remuneration, so that Abd al-Rahman had to rely on the modest income of the several lands in the villages surrounding Aleppo he had inherited from his father. These positions provided Kawakibi with considerable public experience, but also alerted him to the wrongs of the governors and their local accomplices. Therefore, as an intellectual committed to reform, he remained on the other hand loyal to the critical spirit he had demonstrated in his papers, battling against arbitrary rule, corruption, and greed in the name of his class and of the people at large. The government's attitude toward Kawakibi was likewise ambivalent. His defiant activities brought upon him time and again the wrath of the *valis*, who placed him under constant surveillance, repeatedly dismissed him from his posts, and twice arrested him. But then he was reinstated and advanced to the next position.

The two apparently opposite trajectories of Kawakibi's career as a government official and a civil society activist mirrored the inner contradictions of the Hamidian regime, which combined an unprecedented drive for economic and administrative reform with a highly conservative mode of rule. They testified, on the one hand, to the central government's need for modern educated officials created by the Tanzimat reforms, but, on the other hand, to the persistence of its reliance on personal ties and loyalties in carrying out these reforms in the remote provinces. From Kawakibi's viewpoint, these were rather the two complementary avenues open before a reformist Ottoman provincial notable to fulfill his duty for the sake of his country and his people, while at the same time securing a living befitting a man of his standing. His efforts were only hampered by what his friend Kamil al-Ghazzi had identified as two deficiencies in his character: rash impulsivity and reckless boldness. Abd al-Rahman had lofty goals, Ghazzi remarked in a rare critical note, but lacked the patience and moderation needed to attain them. This judgment, as we will see, was not far from the mark. Leaping into every new project without careful planning and with little attention to possible obstacles, Kawakibi would often end up in abject despair.

The outcome of this combination of political circumstances and personal traits was a highly volatile career, in which one post was swiftly replaced by another, alternating between government service and opposition, official favor and persecution. The most important factor in determining Kawakibi's actual standing at a particular moment was his relations with the incumbent governor of Aleppo. A more permanent factor was the evolution of Abdulhamid II's politico-religious policies, against which Kawakibi's reformist thought developed. For the sake of convenience, this checkered career may be roughly divided into three distinct, though often overlapping periods. The dividing lines between them were his two major conflicts with Aleppo's governors, Jamil Pasha in 1886 and Arif Pasha in 1892. In the first period, Kawakibi was still operating as an organic intellectual within the interests of his own notable class; in the second, he moved to an increasingly radical position that represented the people at large in both senses of this term: as the common people of the lower classes, and as the nation, that is, the Arab nation. The third period marks the apex of Kawakibi's career, as he assumed high economic and for the first time also religious positions, but also his downfall. The chapter concludes with a discussion of Kawakibi's short period of exile in Egypt, which ended with his sudden death.

A MAN OF HIS CLASS

Our reconstruction of Abd al-Rahman al-Kawakibi's official career is based on the reproduction of his personal files and other related documents, themselves a mark of the growing bureaucratization of the Ottoman government in the latter part of the nineteenth century. Though not always precise, they provide us with a rough picture of his administrative progress. In March 1878, when already well established as editor of *al-Furat*, Kawakibi was appointed honorary secretary of Aleppo's educational council. A year later, in April 1879, following the final closure of *al-Shahba* and after passing the exams of the council of justice, he was made registrar of the new state's court of first instance, which specialized in the arbitration of local conflicts. Kawakibi was the first to fill this function in Aleppo. In March 1880, perhaps as compensation for the closure of *al-I'tidal*, he also was made honorary member of the educational as well as the public works councils.

About that time, he passed another exam of the justice council and joined the provincial registry office. Later that year, in recognition of his knowledge of the state laws and his contribution to *al-Furat*, he was appointed honorary member of the lawyers' examination council and of Aleppo's press.

Kawakibi's official career received another boost at the beginning of the governorship of Jamil Pasha, who took office in February 1881 and held it for the unusually long period of six years. Jamil began his term with a reshuffle of the administration, dismissing the Muslim and Christian presidents of the city council and many other senior officials. This could enhance the standing of lesser officials such as Kawakibi, who, in March 1881, at the age of twenty-six, was promoted to the office of president of the public works council. In September that year, by order of the ministry of justice in Istanbul, he also was made senior judge in the commercial court. His brother Mas'ud joined the secretariat after him, in 1883, and, unlike Kawakibi, would stick to the post for most of his career. An article by Abd al-Rahman in *al-Furat* of 1884 indicates that, in addition, he held the position of deputy manager of the religious endowments (*awqaf*) in Aleppo. It was his being chief of the provincial registry office, however, that set him on a collision course with the governor, leading first to his resignation from the official paper and later, in late 1886, to his dismissal from all his posts and his first arrest.

Jamil Pasha was the commander of Aleppo's garrison during the harsh winter of 1878–9. His successful handling of the ensuing food riots endeared him to the local notables, who lobbied for his promotion to the provincial governorship. His being the son of Namik Pasha, a former president of the Council of State and a close companion of Sultan Abdulhamid, also helped. Subsequently, he would hold the two offices of governor and military commander of Aleppo. As *vali*, Jamil was very popular with the middle and lower sections of the population. He laid the groundwork for the city's modern education system, renovated dilapidated mosques, improved the urban infrastructure and enhanced the safety of travel throughout the province. These enterprises were capped by the foundation of the lucrative extramural neighborhood that bears his name, al-Jamiliyya.

But, like the Hamidian regime at large, Jamil Pasha had another, less appealing, side, which led the British consul to describe his governorship as "cruel tyranny and infamous iniquity." This was aggravated after Sultan Abdulhamid II began to purchase for himself large estates, which made him one of the largest landowners in the Ottoman Empire. The *vali* seized the opportunity to ingratiate himself with the Sultan, and by the use of force and intimidation procured lands at minimal prices for the imperial farms. In the process, as in all other government transactions, he also enriched himself. By intrigue and fraud, sometimes at the expense of the Sultan himself, Jamil Pasha amassed a huge personal fortune, which he invested throughout the Empire and in Europe. Those who dared stand in his way were arrested, humiliated, and molested.

The principal victim of Jamil Pasha's extortions was the urban notable class, which now could only regret its erstwhile support of his candidacy. In one notorious case, Nafi al-Jabiri, leader of what was by then the most influential notable family in Aleppo and a delegate to the 1877 Ottoman parliament, was exiled for three years because of the family's refusal to give in to the *vali*'s extortions. On his return, Jamil tried to force him to sell a farm for a nominal sum, and when Jabiri tried to escape he was imprisoned and tortured. Another case concerned the Kethuda brothers, who, on the death of their father, one of the richest people in Aleppo at the time and member of the provincial council, were summoned to the *vali*, who demanded a sizable share of the inheritance. The oldest brother was incarcerated until they agreed to pay a hefty ransom for his release. Senior Turkish provincial administrators, and even the foreign consuls and their employees, were not spared such treatment. The general treasurer (*defterdar*) of the province, Emin Effendi, was assaulted and beaten in the street, whereupon a telegraph from Jamil Pasha to the Palace falsely denouncing him for preaching against the Sultan in one of the mosques brought about his immediate dismissal. Hendersson, the British consul, was accused by Jamil Pasha of non-payment of arrears on rent to the *waqf* authorities, while the dragoman of the embassy was subjected to persecution for his refusal to hand over rural lands in his possession.

As inspector of the provincial registry office, Abd al-Rahman al-Kawakibi was best placed to observe the *vali*'s misdeeds. He himself incurred losses when Jamil Pasha sent thugs to destroy and loot the lands on which the family lived. Consequently, Kawakibi took it upon himself to represent the offended leaders of his class. The group would gather in secret at his home and deliberate about the best way to remove Jamil Pasha from office. The result was a barrage of petitions and telegrams enumerating the *vali*'s grave abuses, dispatched through the telegraph office in Aleppo to the Sultan, the Grand Vizier, the interior and justice ministries, and even to Abu al-Huda al-Sayyadi, many of which were formulated in Turkish by Kawakibi himself. He also regularly sent reports on the *vali*'s injustices to the press, and was one of the few inhabitants of Aleppo who ventured to meet the British military attaché who was sent to investigate the *vali*'s quarrels with the consul. The unceasing stream of complaints was apparently a major reason for the Palace's decision, taken in August 1886 after much procrastination, to dispatch a commissioner to Aleppo to inquire into the conduct of Jamil Pasha. The matter seemed serious enough to involve the Sultan himself, who chose for the task the president of the prosecution department in the Council of State, Saib Pasha, a man highly valued for his integrity and capability.

In Aleppo, the heads of the notable families announced that, should the commissioner fail in his duty, they would go to the telegraph office and remain there until the Sultan dismissed Jamil Pasha or suggested another *vilayet* to which all of them could emigrate. The directors of the various administrative offices likewise signed a declaration stating that it was impossible for them to carry out their duties as long as the governor remained in office, and asking to be transferred elsewhere if the Sultan refused to remove him. Kawakibi, who contemplated traveling to Istanbul to present the Kethuda case to the central authorities in person, was summoned by the *vali*, who used abusive language to intimidate him. Subsequently, police broke into the family house and confiscated property, including Kawakibi's printing press, under the pretext of some missing papers in the provincial registry office. In his complaint to the Sultan about the harsh treatment meted out to him, Kawakibi did not fail to point out that he was a descendant of the Prophet and son to one of the most ancient notable families of Aleppo, and that from an early age he had been a loyal servant of the Sultan. He also added that, due to his faith, pedigree, and conduct, he was generally recognized as an erudite scholar and honored man of religion by the people of his city.

Matters came to a head in November 1886. An Armenian lawyer whom Jamil Pasha brought to ruin because he defended the rights of his community attacked the *vali* as his carriage was passing through the new Salimiyya quarter. Exploiting the fact that the lawyer had been an apprentice of Kawakibi, Jamil promptly arrested the latter along with a group of senior notables on the charge of instigating an attempt on his life. The group included the aforementioned Nafi al-Jabiri and Ahmad Kethuda (Kihya), as well as Husam al-Din al-Qudsi, then a member of the provincial council, and other leading notables of Aleppo. The *vali* intended to deport them, but this time he overplayed his hand.

The incident gave Saib Pasha, the Sultan's commissioner who after two months of unfruitful investigations was about to leave, the opportunity to brief the Sultan and inform him about the explosive situation in Aleppo. Abdulhamid was finally persuaded that Jamil Pasha's conduct had become a menace, and he was ordered to depart at once. The notables were acquitted of all charges and released after more than ten days in custody. This happened not before the wives of the arrestees, among them Fatima al-Kawakibi, organized what seems to have been the first women's demonstration in Aleppo.

Upon the arrival of the new *vali*, Osman Nuri Pasha, in Aleppo at the beginning of 1887, Kawakibi was reinstated in the provincial administration. Osman was brought in from the Hijaz, where he had won the special confidence of the Sultan due to his active enhancement of Ottoman rule against the pretentions of the Sharif of Mecca and his supporters among the native Arab tribes. Seeking to draw the restless activist to his side, this exceptionally competent and energetic governor persuaded Kawakibi to assume leadership of the municipality, whose mismanagement he himself had deplored on the pages of *al-I'tidal*. With his usual zeal, the day after his installation, Kawakibi ordered the central market closed to camel traffic for posing a serious danger to the safety of the buyers. At the same time, he began a campaign to eradicate bribery, including a raise in the municipality workers' salary. His measures generated raucous opposition from the wealthy merchants, who saw their interests damaged. Kawakibi was peremptorily dismissed when he refused to pay the *vali* what the latter saw as his due share in the municipality's swelling revenue. As a lesson, Kawakibi was forced to pay from his own pocket the salary increases, as well as the expenses for the fences erected at the market gates to halt the camel traffic. For the next two years, he had to make do with his position as president of the registry office.

FOR THE SAKE OF THE PEOPLE

Abd al-Rahman al-Kawakibi's independent political and social activity complemented his official work, and was particularly intensive when he was out of office. We may gain glimpses of his endeavors for the common people, along with some hints about his patriotic engagement, from the reminiscences of his family and colleagues, as well as from diaries of the foreign consulates in Aleppo. Already at an early age, after he had moved to his own modest house in the Qa'at al-Saqqal quarter, Kawakibi gathered in his salon a group of like-minded friends to discuss the political issues of the day. As we have seen, following the successive closures of his two newspapers, he published anonymous fiery articles in the papers of Istanbul and Beirut against the governors and their administration. These continued to appear intermittently throughout his life in Aleppo.

In 1888, almost a decade after the shattering of his independent journalistic enterprise, Kawakibi resolved to resign from his official positions and embark on a private career. The move took place under the particularly weak and inefficient governorship of Hasan Pasha. Capitalizing on the remarkable success of the campaign to remove Jamil Pasha two years earlier, Kawakibi opened near his house a law office, which specialized in assisting the local people in their dealings with the government and in forwarding petitions against corrupt provincial officials to Istanbul. This time, however, Kawakibi did not confine his services to his own *a'yan* class; on the contrary, he paid special attention to the needs of the poorer sections of the Aleppo population, an activity that gained him the sobriquet "father of the weak" (*abu al-du'afa*). This may have reflected estrangement from the upper notability, people like Nafi al-Jabiri who now ingratiated themselves with the governors and enhanced their interests at the expense of the poor. Kawakibi gave legal advice, arbitrated simple cases, registered objections, and encouraged the offended to send petitions and seek redress directly from the Sultan, the Grand Vizier, or the various ministers in the capital. His office also served other lawyers, and even the government itself, which came to consult him on thorny administrative and legal points.

Kawakibi's legal and social activity was a response to the political transformation taking place in the Ottoman Empire in the second half of the 1880s. At that time, real power was concentrated in the person of Sultan Abdulhamid II, and the provinces came under the direct rule of the Palace. Telegraphic instructions sent regularly in the Sultan's name to the heads of the various branches of the provincial administration overruled the governor's orders. This was accompanied by the ongoing purchase of agricultural lands for the imperial farms, and now also of urban estates. For all that, the central government's ability to control its representatives in the provinces remained limited. People arrested by imperial order languished in prison even when acquitted by the provincial tribunals, appeals on their behalf to the *vali* being to no avail. The Sultan's agents had no qualms about resorting to forcible appropriation and illegal competition in violation of the rights of the villagers and the city dwellers. Such abuses further encouraged the arbitrary conduct and corruption of the local officials, and exacerbated the sufferings of the people. Their deepening anger became channeled by the government propaganda to the restive Armenian community.

The next *vali* of Aleppo, Arif Pasha, who took over in March 1890, was exactly such a type. He had no intention of improving the province's administration and openly accepted gifts and bribes from those seeking lucrative appointments. Kawakibi clashed with him immediately after his arrival over the revenues of a *waqf* property that belonged to him. His persistent complaints against Arif Pasha and his independent activity in

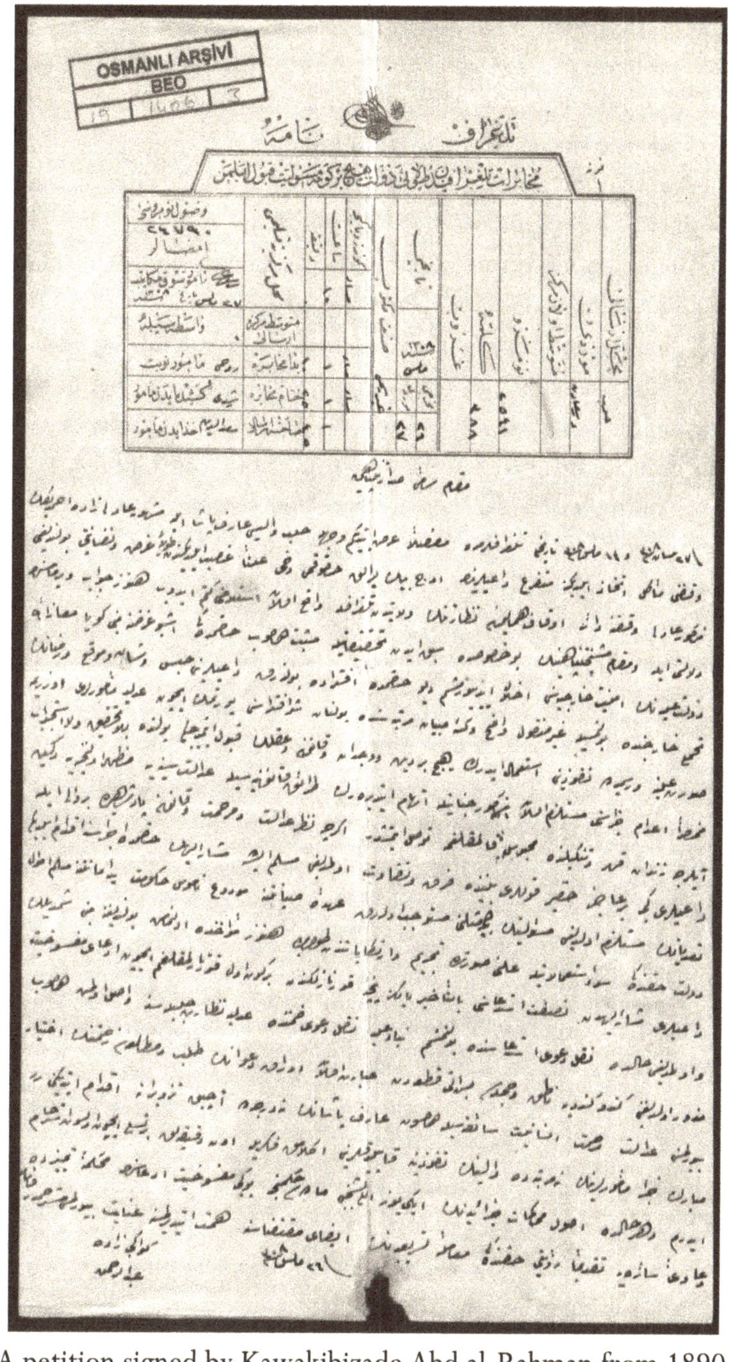

A petition signed by Kawakibizade Abd al-Rahman from 1890

general eventually resulted in his second imprisonment in May 1892. There are at least two versions of this story, which generally bears some resemblance to the first arrest, hence causing some confusion among later biographers. According to one version, Arif Pasha exploited the opportunity of a chance attack on the Italian consul's carriage in the Jallum quarter, where the Kawakibis resided, to implicate Abd al-Rahman in the incident. The governor ordered a report be prepared, to the effect that he belonged to an Armenian band that was behind the assault. The Ottoman authorities in Istanbul were informed that he sent a group of young Muslims to throw stones at the Italian, British, and French consulates in Aleppo as part of an intrigue to bring about the governor's dismissal. The other version has it that some vicious notables, whom Kawakibi denounced for oppressing the poor in complicity with the *vali*, decided to take revenge on him. They paid a policeman to testify that he was intent on setting up an association in opposition to the government.

In any event, Kawakibi's office and house were searched. Fortunately for him, a few minutes before the police arrived at his home, a friend took away his books and papers, including – at least according to his grandson – the draft of his book *The Mother of Cities*. During the search, an incriminating paper was "found" – either a note from an Armenian leader about Kawakibi's intention to steer riots against the Muslims, or a message from himself to the foreign consuls in the city calling on them to oppose the government and rescue the country from its oppression. He was immediately arrested and carried in chains from his home, and under the *vali*'s pressure was indicted for high treason, which carried the death penalty.

Kawakibi appealed to the ministry of justice and managed to have his case transferred to Beirut. There he conducted his own defense, and free of the *vali*'s clutches had little difficulty demonstrating the falsity of the indictment. The Italian consul, meanwhile, submitted a statement to the effect that after an investigation he was quite certain that Kawakibi had no part in the attack on him. The police agents now admitted that no political paper had been found in the search of his house and the "incriminating" document had proven a fake. An article on the affair published in Egypt by his Beiruti friend Abd al-Masih al-Antaki a year after Kawakibi's death shows that he believed that the source of his troubles was no other than Abu al-Huda al-Sayyadi. He is quoted as stating before the court:

> This affliction surrounds me not from now. Its source is Sayyid Abu al-Huda Effendi, who had usurped the *niqabat al-ashraf* of Aleppo from my family. Because I demanded my rights and did not give up, showing more than once in my words and deeds my objection and opposition to him, he became weary and put me in this perilous situation through Arif Pasha, who belongs to his camp. As he found no pretext against me, because I have spent the prime of my life in the service of my state and my nation and my Sultan, he conspired against me with this small paper that they claim to have found among the papers of my children...

Kawakibi was released from prison after eight months and having incurred great expenses, which further strained his financial situation.

A note in the diaries of the French consulate in Aleppo gives the story another twist, indicating that this time much more than the provincial government's corruption was at stake. The note by the consular agent T. Gilbert of 9 July 1892 reports the arrest of Abd al-Rahman [al-Kawakibi] Effendi, head of a secret society, and a certain Sheikh Omer Seifi, the society's secretary. It confirms that a search was conducted among their papers, but then intimates that the most important document seized was a communiqué addressed not to any conspiring Armenian or to the foreign consuls, but to the tribal leaders in the province. It called on them to rebel against the Turks and elect a new Caliph, because the commander of the faithful must be an Arab. To my knowledge, this is indeed the earliest attestation to several major elements – the Bedouins, the Arab Caliphate, and associational activity – that were to find full expression in Kawakibi's scheme of political-religious reform in his magnum opus, *The Mother of Cities*. Nor, according to Gilbert, was this an isolated incident, but one of several of the same nature that indicated the profound antipathy then festering among the Arabs and Kurds of the region toward the Ottoman government.

OVERTURES TOWARD A MIDDLE CLASS

Following his acquittal on all charges in January 1893, Kawakibi returned triumphant to his home in Aleppo. Thousands gathered to welcome him, among them the city notables and the ubiquitous Abu al-Huda al-Sayyadi, who happened to be there. The governor Arif Pasha was disgraced and had to leave, just like his predecessor Jamil Pasha. When the order arrived from Istanbul, a throng of people gathered near the *vali*'s home and drove him off. Osman Nuri Pasha was once again called from the Hijaz to quell the crisis, and soon after his arrival he reinstated Kawakibi in the Ottoman civil service, appointed him again as mayor of Aleppo, and awarded him official decoration and rank. Under Osman's successor, Hasan Pasha, who had also replaced him in his first term in Aleppo, Kawakibi assumed senior judicial and economic posts that marked the pinnacle of his official career. In September 1894, he was appointed by order from Istanbul head secretary of the sharia court. This was followed by his election to the lucrative positions of president of the local Chamber of Commerce and head of the board of directors of the agriculture bank, illustrating the important role he played in the advent of the middle class of Aleppo. In both his official and civic capacities, Kawakibi initiated a series of projects in the city and its environs, including drainage of swamps, bringing fresh water to the city, and electrifying Aleppo as well as Antioch. Each project was to be carried out by a local company. Most projects, however, did not materialize, because of lack of funds, his refusal to pay bribes for the concessions, and local opposition. These failures ultimately led to his resignation from all his posts in mid-1895.

Subsequently, Kawakibi paid his first and only visit to Istanbul. Two years earlier, his brother Mas'ud had been invited to the capital and was made an offer to found a new Arabic-Turkish paper, which he declined. The purpose of Abd al-Rahman's visit is not entirely clear, nor are his whereabouts in the capital. Ghazzi maintains, somewhat contradictorily, that this was a tourist trip aimed at learning first-hand the machinations of the Ottoman tyranny. He also claims that Kawakibi had planned to conceal his identity, but was soon recognized by the informants of Sheikh Abu al-Huda, who invited him to stay at his home. We have no information about the outcome of the visit either, except that his son As'ad stayed behind and enrolled in the military school of medicine, to be joined later by his brother Rashid. This was the school in which the seeds of the Young Turk movement had been sown a few years earlier, while Kawakibi's visit itself coincided with the emergence of the Committee of Union and Progress (CUP), which conspired to depose the Sultan. Two of Kawakibi's articles were published during this period in *Lisan al-Arab* of Alexandria, one of them suggestively titled "That which a man loves most is that which he is forbidden." Another hint at Abd al-Rahman's possible involvement in Young Turk activity while in Istanbul is his grandson's claims that he had actually fled from the Sultan's grip, and that a few days after his return to Aleppo he was attacked by a person who tried to stab him.

Meanwhile, in Aleppo, things began to change after the arrival in late 1895 of the new *vali* Raif Pasha, a former assistant of the great Tanzimat leader Midhat Pasha. During his relatively long term of five years, Raif dedicated himself to the development of the city and to cleansing the administration of bribery. Refusing to follow his predecessor's practice of sending the municipality's taxes to Istanbul, a practice that had greatly hampered Kawakibi's initiatives, Raif Pasha spent them instead on urban projects such as paving streets, enlarging the salubrious suburbs of al-Jamiliyya and al-Aziziyya, creating an artificial lake and gardens, and completing the long overdue new hospital and the carriageway to Alexandretta. Still, the feelings of the more religious-minded inhabitants of Aleppo were offended by the fin-de-siècle open-air cafes that began to crop up in Aleppo offering performances by artists of both sexes, music, and dancing. Moreover, it was in Raif Pasha's time, though by no means his fault, that an Armenian uprising in the northern districts of the province was met by large-scale massacres perpetrated by the Ottoman Hamidiyeh troops and their local aides.

On his return to Aleppo, with an imperial medal, sometime in early 1896, Kawakibi sought to exploit the new circumstances by trying his hand at private business. This may be seen as an attempt to substitute his lesser notable status for a middle-class occupation. He approached the government and was appointed manager of the Régie des Tabacs in the province of Aleppo and the district of Deir al-Zor in exchange for an annual payment in advance. In his usual manner, Kawakibi is said to have defended the rights of the cultivators against corrupt agents and fired officials he deemed inefficient. At the same time, he hired leaders of the bands of smugglers to induce them to stop their trade. He also persuaded some wealthy friends to form a joint-stock company of tobacco under his direction and floated shares to raise money for its operations.

A letter to his son As'ad in Istanbul dated 28 May 1896 gives us a glimpse into Kawakibi's educational philosophy and into the new opportunities for mobilization that presented themselves to the sons of the Ottoman middle class at the end of the nineteenth century. It is particularly illuminating when examined against the education that Ahmad Baha'i al-Kawakibi secured for his sons Abd al-Rahman in the 1860s and Mas'ud in the 1870s (see chapter 1). Kawakibi must have been attracted to the medical profession, as two of his sons became physicians and two more pharmacists. In the letter, he advises his son to follow the example of the European doctors and specialize in one branch of medicine, be it surgery, eye diseases, or brain diseases. Specialization, he pointed out, was the key to fame and success, and might also help him secure a stipend to study in Europe. On the other hand, Kawakibi approves of the broad program of studies at the Military Medical School, and especially recommends the study of Arabic and Turkish composition and of foreign languages, first French and then English, the languages of the professional journals and of politics. At the same time, Kawakibi asks his son not to neglect reading Islamic books of hadith and religious law or Arabic literature, and warns him to adhere to the precepts of his religion and beware of the materialist beliefs circulating in the medical faculty. Still, in contrast to the 1860s, now the modern sciences were at the center of education, while religious studies had moved to the sphere of voluntary self-reading. Concomitantly, the European languages were superseding Turkish, and study in Europe became the coveted goal.

The tobacco company did well at first, especially as Kawakibi managed to lower prices. His new prosperity allowed him to buy from the Qudsis a spacious house in the well-off Farafira quarter. But this project also ultimately ended in failure. This was partly due to the Armenian uprising in 1896 that severely disrupted agricultural production in the northern parts of the province. Kawakibi incurred great losses to himself and to the shareholders, leading Ghazzi to wonder what it was that led an experienced company such as the Régie to surrender its management to a Muslim man of religion! Hounded by the shareholders, and overburdened by the expenses of his new house, Kawakibi had to live on loans, until the return of some confiscated property partly relieved him. The failure of the tobacco enterprise may have played a part in his decision to leave Aleppo for good.

Abd al-Rahman was obliged for the first time to solicit the help of his family branch in Istanbul. In May 1896, through the intervention of Ataullah Pasha al-Kawakibi, then *vali* of Baghdad, who happened to be passing through Aleppo, he regained his post as chief secretary of the sharia court. Kawakibi undertook the position with his usual zeal. He organized the court's timetable and documentation of the proceedings, earmarked a waiting hall, and at his own expense bought curtains to separate the women from the men. At the same time, he headed a commission set up to set compensation for those whose lands were transferred to the imperial farms. After more than two years in the sharia court, however, Kawakibi's enemies managed to persuade Raif Pasha to remove him from office. As compensation, Sheikh Jamaluddin al-Kawakibi, another senior member of the family in Istanbul, secured for him the post of deputy judge in the district of Rashaya in southern Lebanon. Abd al-Rahman declined, and made it known that he intended to travel to Istanbul in order to obtain a more appropriate position. Two weeks before he left, he mortgaged his house in the Farafira quarter and sold some gardens that remained in his possession. Passing through Alexandretta, he boarded a ship that took him to Egypt, never to return.

AN EXILE IN EGYPT

Fleeing from persecution and censorship in their beloved homeland to the freer atmosphere of British Egypt was an experience shared by many a political and religious Arab reformer in the final decades of the Ottoman Empire. To avoid trouble, Abd al-Rahman al-Kawakibi confided his plans to no one. Many years later, Ghazzi recollected how the day before his departure in mid-1898 Kawakibi came to visit him at his home. In retrospect, he claimed that he sensed his friend's intention to escape in order to circumvent the strict Hamidian censorship and publish his book *Umm al-Qura* in Egypt, and somewhat anachronistically that he had warned Kawakibi against publication, lest in light of his reputation as a sharp critic of the government, he would immediately be dubbed a Young Turk and never allowed to return home. Kawakibi insisted that he was only going to Istanbul, but less than two weeks passed before news spread in Aleppo that the articles that would later be published under the title *The Nature of Tyranny* were being printed in Egypt's newspapers.

Abd al-Rahman's grandson, who believed that the Mecca conference actually took place, maintained that there were in fact two trips. The first was to Egypt and the Arabian Peninsula, from which Kawakibi returned to settle his affairs in Aleppo, while the second, with his eldest son Kazim, in May 1900 was for good. But this is improbable as none of Kawakibi's close friends saw him during his supposed one-month stay in the city. In Cairo, he rented a pharmacy for his son, and intended to bring the rest of the family once they were settled. He was warmly welcomed by the Syrian intellectual community of expatriates who preceded him. The group would meet every evening at the Splendid Bar in Cairo and discuss their cherished causes of Islamic reform and Arab freedom from the Turkish yoke. Among them were many leading Salafis and Arabists of the day: Rashid Rida, with whom

Kawakibi cultivated especially close ties, the Damascene reformers Tahir al-Jazairi and Rafiq al-Azm, and the Arabist journalists Muhammad Kurd Ali, Abd al-Qadir al-Maghribi, and Abd al-Hamid al-Zahrawi. Prominent Egyptian colleagues were also involved, including Muhammad Abduh, the doyen of Islamic modernism, who was then Grand Mufti of Egypt and head of the reform council of al-Azhar University, as well as Sheikh Ali Yusuf, editor of the widely circulating *al-Muayyad*, in which *The Nature of Tyranny* first appeared. Kawakibi resided in the vicinity of al-Azhar, dedicating his time to writing and publishing. He seems to have requested a license to publish a new paper called *al-Arab*, but this was denied by the Egyptian authorities who were unwilling to displease the Sultan. The Lebanese journalist Ibrahim Salim al-Najjar claimed in an article published decades later that Kawakibi used to say that if he had an army at his disposal he would at once topple Abdulhamid's government, but this seems implausible, as for him and his generation the Ottomans remained the last mainstay of Muslim power. Rida's testimony that while he praised Abu al-Huda in public he reviled him when speaking to his intimate friends seems much closer to the truth.

Following the publication of *The Mother of Cities*, Kawakibi was approached by Khedive Abbas Hilmi II (r. 1892–1914), who was cultivating his own ambitions for the Caliphate. The Egyptian ruler allocated Kawakibi a monthly stipend of fifty Egyptian pounds as a political refugee and invited him to join him in his negotiations with the Sultan in Istanbul. Apprehensive at Abdulhamid's schemes against him, Kawakibi hesitated and ultimately declined. Instead, he undertook to travel throughout the Arab and Muslim world. Najjar's assertion that these travels were designed to propagate the Khedive's claim to the Caliphate again seems dubious in light of his vision of the Caliphate in *The Mother of Cities*. In 1900, we find Kawakibi touring the coasts of East Africa (visiting Ethiopia, Harrar, Somalia, and possibly Zanzibar) and the southwestern parts of Asia. A year later, he crossed the Arabian Desert on camelback, meeting rulers and tribal leaders of the Peninsula and exploring the region's military, cultural, and economic conditions. His last trip took him as far as Karachi in northwest India, whence he returned aboard an Italian army ship with the help of the Italian political attaché in Muscat, who was a native of Aleppo.

Kawakibi intended to complete his investigations with another trip to West Africa, but did not get the chance to realize it. Three months after his return from India, on the night of 14/15 June 1902, he suddenly died. He had spent the previous day as a guest of the Khedive in Alexandria and remained until late at night with his friends in Café Istanbul. There were rumors, which persist to this day, that Kawakibi was poisoned by agents of Sultan Abdulhamid or of the Khedive Abbas Hilmi, but he apparently suffered a coronary stroke. Obituaries were published in all the major newspapers of Egypt, reflecting the high respect and esteem he gained during the short time he had spent in Egypt. As soon as the news of Kawakibi's death reached Istanbul, Abd al-Qadir al-Qabbani, editor of the Beirut Muslim paper *Thamarat al-Funun* and Kawakibi's close friend, was dispatched to Cairo to seize his papers and send them immediately to the Palace. Kawakibi was buried in a modest cemetery at the foot of the Muqattam hill in a religious ceremony at the personal expense of the Khedive and in the presence of many of his Syrian and Egyptian friends and colleagues.

4

THE CRISIS OF THE MUSLIM WORLD

KAWAKIBI'S OEUVRE

Apart from the short-lived independent journalistic experience at the beginning of his career in the late 1870s, and the occasional articles he published, usually anonymously, in other newspapers during the 1880s and 1890s, Abd al-Rahman al-Kawakibi's literary work is concentrated in two books. Both were published toward the end of his life, in 1900, in Egypt under the pseudonym *al-Rahhala* (the great traveler) *K*. One book is *The Mother of Cities* (Umm al-Qura [Mecca]), which sums up from a religious point of view his insights gleaned from his quarter-of-a-century stormy career in the Ottoman provincial town of Aleppo. The other, *The Nature of Tyranny and the Injuries of Enslavement* (Taba'i' al-istibdad wa-masari' al-isti'bad), which is the foremost exposition of Kawakibi's political teaching, reflects his disappointment at Sultan Abdulhamid II's regime, which came to the fore following his visit to Istanbul. The two works are complementary, sometimes repeating the same ideas and arguments, but they nevertheless differ in perspective.

There are allusions to the existence of other works by Kawakibi that were seized upon his death and have since disappeared. These were in different stages of writing and apparently further elaborated upon his religio-political vision. One is *The Quraysh Papers* (Saha'if Quraysh), which he promised to publish as a sequel to *The Mother of Cities* to deal with the scholarly and moral renaissance of Islam. His son As'ad maintained that it was almost ready for publication. Another work is the politically oriented *Greatness Is to God* (al-Azama li-llah), the introduction to which the Syrian nationalist Muhammad Kurd Ali claimed to have seen in Egypt; and there are also notes from his travels and from a study on genealogy. Three years after Kawakibi's death, *al-Manar* published a chapter from another study on slavery in Islam, which was inspired by his promise to return his children's nursemaid to her family in Sudan and included observations from the slave market in Jeddah and a call to end this ignoble practice. Like other men of religion of his day, Kawakibi also tried his hand at poetry, some examples of which are found in *Umm al-Qura*.

There is some uncertainty as to the circumstances in which Kawakibi composed his two surviving books, and considerable differences of opinion about the measure of their originality. Both works apparently had been conceived successively in his study in Aleppo, where he regularly read the Turkish and Egyptian papers that circulated in the city despite the official ban; both also bear witness to the influence of his discussions and debates with fellow Syrian and Egyptian reformers in the freer atmosphere of British Egypt. Still, while *The Mother of Cities* was written in the main while he was still in Aleppo, the writing of *The Nature of Tyranny* was deferred until after the move to Egypt. In both books, Kawakibi, as he himself readily admitted, borrowed from others: the Young Ottomans, the proponents of the Arab *nahda*, and Westerners. One can hardly deny, however, his compelling style, the breadth of his synthesis, and the new ideas he explored, which established his fame as a pioneer of Islamic democracy and socialism, Arab nationalism and the Arab

Caliphate, and, last but not least, the separation of religion from politics.

The following three chapters are dedicated to Kawakibi's mature teaching. The discussion of *The Mother of Cities* is divided into two parts (chapters 4 and 5), the first concerning his diagnosis of the afflictions of the Muslim world, the second his schemes for reform. Chapter 6 deals with *The Nature of Tyranny*. The views expounded in each of his two major works are examined from two perspectives: first, in the light of the ideas Kawakibi had expressed at the beginning of his career in the journals *al-Shahba* and *al-I'tidal* (analyzed in chapter 2) and against the background of his subsequent public career in Aleppo (chapter 3). Second, they are examined in relation to the Islamic reformist thought of the time. The first perspective is designed to trace the changes in Kawakibi's mature thought, while the second is meant to bring into relief both the common ground he shared with other Islamic reformers and Arab proto-nationalists and his original contributions. A comparative look at the two different versions of *The Nature of Tyranny* will add some clues as to development of Kawakibi's ideas during his stay in Egypt.

AN ISLAMIC CONFERENCE IN MECCA

The Mother of Cities was written for the most part during the 1890s in Aleppo. Colleagues such as Kamil al-Ghazzi and Raghib al-Tabbakh testified that they and others in their intellectual circle had seen the manuscript time and again. As we have mentioned, Ghazzi claimed he warned him not to publish it, but Kawakibi paid little heed to the advice. He continued to work on the manuscript after arriving in Egypt until it appeared in 1900. *The Mother of Cities* was published originally under the title *Sijjil mudhakkirat jam'iyyat Umm al-Qura* (Protocol of Deliberations of the Association of the Mother of Cities), which Kawakibi insisted had actually existed; two years later, it was serialized in *al-Manar*, the Islamic journal of Rashid Rida, who then published it with his own annotations in 1904. The latter version underwent some revision, in which passages deemed by the editor too critical of the Ottoman government were excised. A second edition appeared in Aleppo in 1959 with a brief preface by the author's grandson and namesake Dr. Abd al-Rahman al-Kawakibi, but this is practically identical to the original.

The Mother of Cities was composed in a peculiar literary form. It is framed as the protocol of the meetings, deliberations, and decisions of an imaginary conference held in Mecca on the eve of the pilgrimage season of 1899. Twenty-three distinguished Muslim leaders were invited to take part, though one of them, the man of letters from Beirut, for some unspecified reason was unable to attend. This may allude to Kawakibi's fellow journalist and friend Abd al-Qadir al-Qabbani, or any other intellectual who was constrained to remain in Lebanon and face the Hamidian censorship. The conference is purported to be secret, and to that end a special house was rented on the outskirts of Mecca, and a long numerical code was devised to conceal the identity of its members, yet to be deciphered. At its end, it was decided that some deliberations would remain undisclosed. The book contains detailed protocols of the first eight sessions, a final set of rules that came out of the remaining four sessions, an appendix, an afterword, and some notifications, including another alphabetical code of a message that "time will reveal."

Once convened, each participant in the imaginary Mecca conference was given a distinct appellation, which again leaves room for speculation as to its meaning and identity. Some of the appellations are fairly straightforward, such as the Mujtahid of Tabriz, who is a Shi'i jurist, or the *shaykh* from Sind, who is a Sufi master. Others seem to convey a message. The most general title, that of religious scholar (*'alim*), is bestowed on the representative of Najd, home of the Wahhabi movement in central Arabia, while the representative of England, and by implication of the West at large, is called the felicitous (*sa'id*). Together, these leaders represent most important Muslim communities of the time – from India and China in the east to Tunisia and Morocco in the west. Still, more than half of the participants are of Arab stock, while the fringes of Southeast Asia, Sub-Saharan Africa or the Americas are represented only indirectly or not at all.

The convener and secretary of the Mecca conference was *al-Sayyid al-Furati*, who is no other than Kawakibi himself, the scion of the Prophet and editor of Aleppo's official paper, *The Euphrates*. The chairman of the meetings is by the nature of things the representative of Mecca, although significantly his appellation is the rather modest *ustadh*, which basically means teacher. Finally, while the participants purport to express different viewpoints – regional, sectarian, or theological – it is actually Kawakibi who speaks through them all. Together, they reflect his views on the current appalling situation of the Muslim world and his call for religious reform that will return Islam to its original glorious days under the guidance of the Arabs, and thereby attain a leading position in the modern world.

The literary form of *The Mother of Cities* serves Kawakibi in a number of related ways. First, the assembly of Muslim leaders from all over the world in Mecca during the pilgrimage season signifies one of the pillars of his religious reform, namely the unity of Islam. In this respect, he proves himself a follower of the pan-Islamic schemes that were advanced in the last part of the nineteenth century by both the Islamic revolutionary Jamal al-Din al-Afghani and the absolutist Sultan Abdulhamid II.

Kawakibi makes room for the Shi'a in this unity, and, unlike any of the Islamic reformers of his time, he even gives it pride of place in his program for the overall revival of Islam. Also unlike them, the unity he suggests aims at the spiritual regeneration of the umma rather than its actual political unification. I could find no evidence that Kawakibi was among the recipients of Afghani and Abduh's influential early Islamic journal *The Firmest Bond* (al-Urwa al-wuthqa) in 1884, when he was engaged in the struggle against the oppressive governor Jamil Pasha, or to any meeting between him and Afghani, by that time an eventual prisoner of the Sultan, when he visited Istanbul in 1895–6.

Second, the mode of analyses and debates that fill the protocols of the meetings point to another major principle of Kawakibi's religious reform, namely rational deliberation. Following in the footsteps of the young Ottomans, he is keen to demonstrate that Muslim regeneration cannot be effected simply by coercion from above, in the manner followed with mixed results by the Tanzimat reformers; it also must take into consideration the opinions of perceptive men of religion, leaders of the community, and political thinkers, as was the case in the short-lived Ottoman parliament of 1876, which he had so fervently supported. In this respect, the Mecca conference amounts to a call to establish a public sphere in the Habermasian sense of an ideal arena in which knowledgeable men meet to discuss on an equal footing in a critical-rational manner the affairs of society and state. Kawakibi anchors this call in the Quranic principle of consultation (*shura*), which by implication includes the European-derived right of assembly and the freedoms of speech and publication. The secrecy in which the conference was held, though part of the book's charm, is indicative of the very lack of these rights and freedoms in the Ottoman Empire, where persecution by state officials, formidable censorship, and the ignorance of the masses were the rule.

Last but not least, in the breadth of the knowledge and the force of the analysis he displays through the mouths of the participants, Kawakibi embodies the new class of religious intellectuals that emerged in the Ottoman Empire in the wake of the Tanzimat reforms. The first generation of modern Islamic reformers from the urban centers of Syria, Iraq, and Egypt were versed in the traditional religious sciences, but they were also eager to acquire the secular sciences and alert to the political and social realities of their time, interests they shared with their non-Muslim compatriots. These new intellectuals strove to carve out a place for themselves in the power structure of the fledgling modern Muslim state by forging ideologies that would enable the Muslim community and the Arab *ethnie* to embrace Western ideas and institutions without losing their identity and self-respect. Kawakibi's efforts in this direction constitute a significant contribution to the two major ideologies that shaped Middle Eastern politics during the twentieth century: Islamic reform and Arab nationalism.

More generally, the style of the deliberations and decisions, the order and manner of their presentation, and their division into debates, sessions, reports, and regulations are an integral part of the content of the Mecca conference. To recall communications expert Marshall McLuhan's famous dictum, in this case too, the medium is the message. These features provide us with important clues to Kawakibi's thought and constitute an additional key to the encoding of the mysteries of his text.

THE DEGENERATION OF THE UMMA

The imaginary Islamic conference in Mecca was convened by Abd al-Rahman al-Kawakibi to look into the reasons behind the degeneration of the Muslim peoples (to be dealt with in this chapter) and suggest ways for the reform of Islam (the topic of the next chapter). In the medical vocabulary typical of the religious reformist discourse of the time, it aimed to cure the weakness and malady, the lethargy and paralysis that had afflicted the Muslim umma. The distinguished participants swear at the opening session before Almighty God to exert their utmost effort (*jihad*) to make His word supreme and to be loyal (*amana*) to their Muslim brethren, those who profess His unity. Theirs, therefore, is not Afghani's call to unite in armed struggle against European colonialism, but more in tune with the later Abduh's intellectual striving to enlighten the Muslim community.

The mission that Kawakibi sets for the Mecca conference is fourfold: to alert the Muslims to their grave situation, point to ignorance as its underlying cause, warn of the dire consequences, and denounce those who obstruct unity, be they the rulers, the religious class, or the common people. More specifically, he formulates ten guiding questions to be considered by the participants in their deliberations. The first five refer to the problem, or malady, of the Muslim umma; the other five are designed to show the way to the solution. In the latter questions, Kawakibi uses the neologism *islamiyya*, which may be rendered as Islamism. By this, as we shall see, he means the original Islam of the Prophet and the forefathers, which for him is equivalent to the modern ideal of government and society based on liberty, equality, justice, and reason. Islamism is set against other religions, especially the Christian denominations of Catholicism and Protestantism, but it actually denotes Islamic ideology.

In remarkable continuity with his early journalist style, Kawakibi resorts time and again to history to press his point. This is evident even in regard to the conference itself. The degeneration of Islam had become apparent more than a millennium ago, says the Meccan teacher in his inaugural speech after his election as chairman, that is, right after the age of the *salaf*. The situation continuously deteriorated down the centuries, he continues, until other nations – the Europeans – took the lead. They excelled in the arts and sciences, augmented their power and extended their influence over most Muslim as well as non-Muslim countries around the world. Today, in the heyday of colonialism, they are approaching the very heart of Islam: the Arabian Peninsula. This danger, the chairman maintains, is what has finally awakened the more conscious among the Muslims – the new religious intellectuals, who have joined in the effort to revive Islam. As their movement is still feeble and their thoughts confused, it is the task of this conference to help unite and empower them, and through them the entire umma.

The view of the Muslim world that emerges from the pages of *The Mother of Cities* is bleak indeed. Gone is the guarded optimism of *al-Shahba* and *al-I'tidal*. Kawakibi now characterizes the situation in the harshest words as a general enervation, which like an infectious disease has spread throughout the Islamic "body" and made Muslims everywhere and in almost every respect inferior to their non-Muslim neighbors. The range of possible causes of the Muslim degeneration suggested by the participants in the course of two full sessions of the Mecca conference, which reflects the variety of opinions prevalent among the Islamic reformers of the time, is bewildering. Some explanations are doctrinaire, others practical; some are religious and some political, or social and economic; most have deep roots in the past while a few are more recent. They are raised, and debated, without apparent order, a literary means that, apart from demonstrating what a civil critical-rational debate should be like, also allows Kawakibi to convey to his readers the complexity of the situation and the difficulty of finding out its root cause.

Among the reasons suggested for the current Muslim degeneration are belief in predestination and encouragement of the ascetic way of life; the transformation of Muslim politics from the democracy of the rightly guided Caliphs to an absolutist kingdom; the ignorance and inaction of pleasure-loving rulers; the idleness and frivolity of the general public; neglect of the Divine commandment to forbid the wrong (*al-nahi 'an al-munkar*); dissolution of the religious bond; the enchantment by sham men of religion and extremist Sufis of rulers and masses alike; the corruption and despotism of the government; the domination by the official ulama, who are nothing but turbaned ignoramuses; the Muslim scholars' preoccupation with the religious sciences at the expense of the exact and natural sciences; recoil from competition with the other nations; loss of true leaders and guides; lack of capital, and mass poverty; the absence of deliberation and consultation among the Muslims; and the venality of the rulers who rely on sycophantic men of religion.

While most of the discussion is couched in general terms, Kawakibi's principal concern was clearly with the Ottoman state of his day, which for him represented the depths of Muslim decay. Eventually, there was one specific issue on which he was apparently no longer able to restrain himself, and made his implicit indictment open: the self-seeking men of religion. It is also not difficult to gauge whose figure he had in mind – it was no other than his archenemy the Grand Sufi of the Ottoman Empire, Sheikh Abu al-Huda al-Sayyadi. The lawyer participant from Medina asserts that the cause of the calamity is fake ulama and extravagant Sufis, who captured religion and brought it to ruin. In Constantinople:

> These swindlers attained through their sorcery tremendous influence, by which they corrupted much of the religion, turning schools into lodges for the idle who falsely testify to their frightening miracles, and mosques into meeting places for drummers who rock the hearts of those in doubt and darken their nerves ... making the alms tax (*zakat*) of the community and its inheritances into their livelihood, and the income of the religious endowments (*awqaf*) of kings and princes into gifts to their followers.

The Anatolian master follows suit when he describes how, by endearing themselves to the rulers, these turbaned boors were able to devise a special regulation for themselves, which made the religious sciences an official gift to be conferred on illiterates and children, inherited, and even bought and sold on the job market. The damage done by these imposters was threefold: they charmed the Muslim masses away from their religion, shattered the reputation and livelihood of the righteous ulama, and whispered in the ears of the rulers to ignore the advice of their people. It is these observations that led Kawakibi to depart from his early preoccupation with Ottoman politics and turn his gaze to the religion of Islam.

CRITIC OF THE RELIGIOUS TRADITION

Kawakibi's view of the present state of Muslim religiosity is articulated in the Mecca conference through the mouth of the Najdi scholar. By this means, he alludes to the close affinity of his ideas to those of the Wahhabis, not the original movement of the second half of the eighteenth century that declared other Muslims unbelievers and defied the Ottoman Sultan's authority, but rather its late nineteenth-century heirs, who relinquished its original militancy while keeping to its strict adherence to the Quran and the Sunna of the Prophet. Kawakibi refers to the people of central Arabia, together with the Zaydis of Yemen, as adherents of the Salafi creed. Summing up the deliberations so far, the Najdi scholar "asserts, not merely thinks or surmises, that the [root] cause of the slackness that has befallen this religious community is the present religion itself." "Does any doubt remain after the investigations we have heard in our conference," he asks rhetorically, "that today's religion, in terms of what we believe and practice, not of what we profess and say, is not the religion that distinguished our ancestors (*aslafina*)?" The blame lies on the successors (*al-akhlaf*), who have overlooked many fundamental provisions of the scriptures, while adding unauthorized innovations and unfounded superstitions. The huge edifice of the tradition they have thus erected throughout the later ages often impinges upon the foundations of the religion, and at times on its very foundation, the unity of God.

The Najdi scholar's speech, which stretches over almost the entire fourth session, and continues with a question and answer section into the fifth, sets out from two preambles that combine reason with faith. The rational side, which is more typical of Abduh and his school than of the Wahhabis, is designed to prove the existence of God and the need for prophets to guide humanity on questions that the intellect is incapable of comprehending. Without such guidance, he argues, people are prone to associate others with God (*shirk*), imagining them as all sorts of intermediaries invested with divine powers and hidden knowledge. On the religious side, the Najdi scholar stresses the Muslim belief that Muhammad was the last and perfect messenger sent to all humanity, and that it is incumbent upon the believers to strictly follow the precepts of the

Quran and the Sunna, rather than rely on their own opinion. The latter observation, however, is significantly qualified by the claim that only unequivocal rulings in the scriptures must be thus obeyed, a fact that leaves ample room for reason and agency in worldly affairs.

Like other religious reformers of the late nineteenth century who followed the Wahhabis on this point, Kawakibi's Salafi critique of the Muslim tradition focuses on the two major domains of Sufism and jurisprudence. From the Najdi scholar's point of view, the whole gamut of popular practices associated with Sufism is nothing but polytheism. He condemns visitations to saints' tombs and asking their favors; excessive veneration of living sheikhs; the *dhikr* ceremonies; the esoteric sciences, which are based on allegorical interpretations of ambiguous Quranic verses and unreliable hadith; and new rituals with no foundation in the scriptures. He thus proclaims:

> Among them are people who hang on the walls of their houses and even of their mosques tablets naming their venerated ones resembling the tablets for images among Christians and idolaters. They invoke them for blessing, remembrance, and supplication. Through them they turn to the luminaries like this: "Oh Ali, Oh Shadhili, Oh Dasuqi, Oh Rifa'i, Oh Baha' al-Din al-Naqshi, Oh Jalal al-Din al-Rumi, Oh Bektash Veli."

No less reprehensible in Kawakibi's eyes are the use of singing and dancing, beating drums, playing with swords and fire, and eating live scorpions and snakes among the popular Sufis, and the pretentions of all sorts of spiritual "experts" to fortune telling, healing, and divination with the help of the jinn and the spirits. These practices have turned religion into a plaything and fraud, he complains, dragging the Muslim umma back to the days of pre-Islamic barbarity (*jahiliyya*), the ultimate expression of the natural human inclination to disbelief.

Somewhat surprisingly for a Wahhabi follower, the Najdi scholar holds that the greatest fault of the jurists lies in the excessive strictness of their legal methods, which, contrary to God's explicit intention, have turned religion into an unbearable yoke. He rebukes them for opting for the most severe interpretation whenever there are seeming contradictions in the text of the Quran, of reaching far-fetched conclusions from inconsequential actions or words of the Prophet, and of adding restrictions and prohibitions only to demonstrate their faith and piety. Such methods, he contends, create difficulties and confusion among the common believers and lead them to neglect their religion altogether or turn to the popular Sufis.

THE FAILINGS OF THE TANZIMAT

Kawakibi's view of the Ottoman government and society of his day is reserved for the final part of the deliberations at the Mecca conference, just before moving to the actual resolutions. Significantly, it is articulated through the convener of the conference, *al-Sayyid al-Furati*, the appellation of Kawakibi himself, in a speech that stretches over two full sessions (7 and 8) and amounts to a scathing censure of the Ottoman course of reform. Echoing the constitutional ideas of the Young Ottomans, which had already animated his early articles in *al-Shahba* and *al-I'tidal*, he traces the appalling condition of the Ottoman Empire to the political and administrative misgovernment that had afflicted it mainly in the previous sixty years, that is, since the inauguration of the Tanzimat reforms in 1839. These, he claims, led to the neglect of the old principles without adequate appropriation of new ones. The state of the Empire has further deteriorated in the previous twenty years, he adds, which corresponds to his own career under Abdulhamid II's rule, during which two-thirds of the Ottoman territory was lost and the remaining third destroyed, as the Sultan spent all its remaining energy in protecting himself and maintaining his despotic rule.

The list of deficiencies of the Tanzimat regime enumerated by Kawakibi, which reflects his own experience as well as the discussions held in the salons of the new intellectuals of Aleppo, is again bewildering. Among them are the standardization of administrative and legal rules without regard for differences among the various elements of the Empire, excessive centralization of government, inappropriate appointments and irresponsibility on the part of governors and high officials, racial inequality, discrimination in matters of taxation and fines, lack of reward for good work and suppression of innovative ideas in the administration, indifference to religious laws and customs, mismanagement of the budget leading to indebtedness to foreigners, ruling by deceit and silencing rather than by consultation, and servile flattery and bribery of the Western powers.

These facets in the maladministration of the Empire are augmented by another set of factors that mark the failure of the promise of the Tanzimat reformers to assimilate modern notions and institutions to the benefit of the Empire and its subjects. One such factor is associated with the idea of ethnic nationalism. Kawakibi blames the Ottoman Turks for their inability to reconcile themselves with the morals and customs of their Arab subjects, which in his view derives from their hatred of and contempt for the Arabs. Another is related to the notion of self-discipline. He complains that people don't bother to learn a profession and have no idea how to arrange their time or balance their budget.

One last important factor that Kawakibi attributes to the failures of the Tanzimat touches on the status of women. He subscribes to the accepted view of his time that women cunningly use their charms to rule over men and therefore must be segregated at home and cover their faces in public. But he also cites the sharia demand for harmony in couples to argue in favor of their education on the same level as men. Like his contemporary Qasim Amin, the champion of women's emancipation in Egypt, Kawakibi saw female illiteracy as a principal source of the malaise of Muslim society. Ignorant women, he claims, would never let their husbands be courageous and manly, nor would they implant in their sons lofty inclinations that lead to glorious deeds. This has resulted in a sense of weakness and inferiority, which spreads from old men to the young and from the upper class to all strands of society. Such men humiliate themselves before their superiors and imitate foreigners to the point of abandoning their religion and feeling ashamed of their origins. This, Kawakibi maintains, is particularly harmful for the youth, on which the hopes and dreams of the fatherland and the nation are pinned. Adopting Western ideas and forms without due regard, Muslim youth suffer from lack of values, neglect their religion, and live in indiscipline, idleness, and sycophancy.

Abd al-Rahman al-Kawakibi's scathing critique of the Muslims' condition at the end of the nineteenth century is set forth in *The Mother of Cities* along two interlocking lines. From the religious standpoint, he joins the other Salafis of the time in attributing the degeneration of the umma to the deviations of the Muslim tradition as it evolved down the ages, especially its two major pillars of popular Sufism and conservative jurisprudence. From the political standpoint, Kawakibi follows the Young Ottomans in censuring the high-handed and flawed administration of the Tanzimat reforms, and their accentuation under Abdulhamid II's despotic regime. These two lines of criticism meet in the sycophantic men of religion who, epitomized in the figure of the Sultan's Sufi advisor Sheikh Abu al-Huda al-Sayyadi, flatter the rulers while fostering the ignorance and servility of the masses. It is primarily against these sham men of religion that Kawakibi sets out to formulate his scheme for reform.

5

A BLUEPRINT FOR REFORM

MODERNIST SALAFI REFORMATION

At the heart of the religious reform suggested by Kawakibi and his fellow Salafis was the return to the original Islam of the scriptures, as these were understood and practiced by the pious early generations (*al-salaf al-salih*). For him, in particular, it was also the Islam still practiced among the inhabitants of the Arabian Peninsula. The principles of this enlightened form of Salafism were enshrined in the very rules of discussion at the Mecca conference as these were spelled out by the chairman in his inaugural speech:

> Brothers! I believe that you will approve of putting aside the differences of the schools of law (*madhhabs*) which we are accustomed to follow blindly (*taqlid*) as we do not know the sources of many of their rulings, and that we will rely on what we know is the clear Quran, the correct Sunna and firm consensus (*ijma'*). Thus our opinions will not be divided and our decisions will be accepted by all Muslims. The school of the ancestors (*madhhab al-salaf*) is the undisputed root and the community of believers will never oppose returning to it and agreeing on some cardinal questions on this foundation.

Kawakibi's call to return to the scriptures is thus grounded in two considerations. One is their truth value, the other their utility as arbiter among different opinions, and hence as the harbinger of unity. To this is added a second, complementary, principle, which involves human agency and reason. As the chairman sums up his point: "I see no hindrance in dropping the divergent opinions, especially those that depend on scant evidence, and agree to return to what *we understand* from the scriptures, or what *according to our abilities* seems to have been the way of the ancestors" [my emphases].

The truth value of the scriptures is a matter of faith. The preservation of the Quran without any corruption and change is part of its wondrous nature (*i'jaz al-qur'an*), claims Kawakibi. The Sunna likewise came down the ages with complete accuracy, particularly through the six canonical collections. Both have won the consensus of the umma. Still, unlike the Wahhabis or purist Salafis today, for Kawakibi, the return to the scriptures does not mean total rejection of either the juristic tradition or the Sufi aspect of Islam. Despite his scathing critique of their current practices, for substantive and utilitarian reasons, he believed that both religious fields should be corrected rather than eliminated. The issue of their reform in the light of the scriptures and the forefathers' example comes up time and again in the course of the deliberations at the Mecca conference, clearly evincing their importance in his eyes.

In the field of jurisprudence, Kawakibi recognized the unavoidability of the differences of opinion. As the Najdi scholar, who represents contemporary Wahhabis, explains at the end of his long speech, these derive from ambiguous passages in the scriptures, different methods of ruling, and diverse ways of implementation; fortunately, he adds, such differences touch on matters of detail and not on the fundamentals of religion, and they relate only to human relations rather than to the worship of God. Two distinct ways are offered by Kawakibi to further mitigate their harm, one innovative, the other long established. For the Egyptian luminary, who lives in one of the most advanced Muslim countries in terms of education and freedom of press, the way to reform passes through the codification of the law books within the schools, so that everyone can easily find what is forbidden and what is permitted by his religion. Kawakibi could draw the idea from the Ottoman project of codifying the official Hanafi law, the Mecelle. The hadith transmitter from Yemen, by contrast, relies on the ancient system that has been preserved in his backward country. Pointing out that his countrymen follow the Zaydi and Hanbali schools, he maintains that correct religion is upheld by the hierarchical division of society into three ranks: the scholars, who derive rulings directly from the scriptures; readers possessing general knowledge and understanding; and the common people, who follow the guidance of the scholars by way of persuasion and proof rather than by mere imitation.

Sufism is subject to much harsher treatment at the hands of Kawakibi, as of the Salafis in general. Its representative at the Mecca conference, the Sindhi sheikh, is a master in the Naqshbandi brotherhood, one of the most orthodox and activist mystical traditions, who spread the path in India and Central Asia, as well as in the Ottoman lands. He is made to confess before his colleagues that their words made him realize that Sufi practices, such as the *dhikr* ceremony, concentration on the spiritual guide and supplication of the prophets and righteous, smack of unlawful innovation (*bid'a*) and polytheism (*shirk*). Repenting, he vows to work with great care to correct his disciples. Still, Kawakibi does not deny the merits of the "true" Sufis, those who follow the way of the ancestors and immerse themselves in worshiping God, purifying their souls, and avoiding the pleasures of this world for the sake of the next. He simply claims that such Sufis have become extremely rare, since the early ascetics have been replaced by pagan-inspired metaphysicians and self-appointed imposters.

Kawakibi knew that neither the codification of the sharia nor self-restraint on the part of the Sufis was an adequate means for meeting the rising challenge of modernity. The reform of Islam also required accommodation of the Western model, especially the adoption of its scientific-rationalist method. This is presented to the Mecca conference through an imaginary report, imagination within imagination, of a dispute that took place between a Russian Orientalist who had recently converted to Islam and the Mufti of Kazan. The Orientalist is the prototypical scholar as he both dedicates himself to the study of Islam and embraces it as the ultimate truth. In the discussion, he expresses his desire to follow the path of the Quran and the reliable Sunna according to his understanding and ability, while the mufti tries desperately to defend the tradition. Using rational rather than scholastic arguments, the Orientalist sees no logic in accepting the authority of the traditional jurists, since their contradictory rulings annul each other. He likewise rejects seniority and popularity as measures of truth, since in this case paganism and Christianity will be deemed superior to Islam, and he defies adherence to one particular school of law on the grounds that this entails multiple Divine justices and knowingly obeying wrong rulings.

The major legal obstacle in the way of reform in Kawakibi's view is thus blind imitation within the schools of law. As the Orientalist declares, "God knew what is best in what He decreed for your guidance, but He left you the choice by way of permission in all other matters in order that you adapt them to the needs of the time, the father of all change, and the requirements of the circumstances, which never stay still." Rigidity under the rule of the clergy, he maintains, was the cause of the decline of Talmudic Judaism and Catholic as well as Orthodox Christianity, whereas Protestantism, by calling for a return to the origins, opened the door to the sciences and arts. Like other Modernist Salafis of his time, Kawakibi assured his readers that Islam does not contradict reason and science, and that all facts revealed through scientific research are already mentioned, explicitly or implicitly, in the Quran. His trust in modern science is such that he lets the Orientalist declare:

> I believe that within less than a century many Orientalists will embrace Islam and take it upon themselves to liberate the sharia and spread it among humanity and its people of standing. It is not unlikely that time will produce an English or Russian prince Muhammad who will be guided to fill the place of the Imam and restore in perfect order the glory of Islam.

To offset the evils of blind imitation, the Modernist Salafis resorted to and revamped the legal mechanism of *ijtihad*. Broadening its semantic field from the mere effort to find an appropriate ruling to independent judgment, they made this concept the cornerstone of both the rationalization and the unity of Islam. This brought them closer to the Shi'a, in which *ijtihad* has long been the accepted practice, and may help explain the particular spell that the Shi'i-born Afghani cast on many a Sunni reformer. Kawakibi apparently went further than any of his Salafi colleagues in his readiness to welcome the Shi'a into the fold of Islam. In *The Mother of Cities*, the Mujtahid of Tabriz, in northwestern Iran, identifies two major calamities that afflicted Islam. One was the first civil war following the murder of Othman in 656, which began as a bid for the Caliphate and ended in the great religious schism between Sunna and Shi'a. The second calamity resulted from the intervention of the Abbasid caliphs in theological matters, the infamous mid-ninth-century inquisition (*mihna*). This, he maintains, fostered casuistry and hostility among the scholars and wiped out many of their schools of law, leaving only six: the four Sunni schools and the (Twelver) Shi'i and Zaydi ones. Kawakibi hence saw no essential difference between Sunnis and

Shi'is; their split was merely a historical accident which the reform of Islam must heal.

On the other hand, Kawakibi is careful to point out that the Shi'i practice of *ijtihad* is not unlimited. The Iranian scholars, the participant from Tabriz explains, are the followers of the *madhhab* of the sixth Imam, Jaf'ar al-Sadiq. Contrary to what the Sunnis think of them, they do not pass independent judgment on the foundations of religion, nor do they allow personal opinion when there is general consensus, or conjecture that has no basis in the sayings of the ancestors. Moreover, in case of difficulty, when the Ja'fari rulings are patently unsuitable, the Shi'i *mujtahids* prefer the rulings of other schools, a legal practice that is called *talfiq* (patching up). Kawakibi is inclined to expand the semantic meaning of this concept, too, and permit, as did Muhammad Abduh, Afghani's principal disciple in Egypt, blending the rulings of the different schools in case of need. This was essential, he believed, to prevent excessive partisanship to one school of law and to foster the unity of the umma.

On the issue of the reform of Sufism, Kawakibi allows himself once more to be much more radical. He suggests imposing on each brotherhood a specific task in the service of the Muslim nation: caring for orphans, assisting the poor, calling people to prayer, preaching against the consumption of intoxicating drinks and other lawful good works.

THE MODEL OF THE WEST

The call to return to the example of the *salaf*, and the complementary injunction to implement it in the light of contemporary readings of the scriptures by way of *ijtihad*, makes room for the critical adoption of modern ideas and values coming from the West. First among these in *The Mother of Cities* is the idea of liberty, one of the pillars of Young Ottoman thought, which Kawakibi had embraced from the very beginning of his career, when he tried to be elected to the first Ottoman parliament in 1876. For him, we may recall, the Islamic politics of the rightly guided Caliphs was nothing but representative and cooperative democracy, before it degenerated under their successors into an absolutist kingdom. "Who will teach us what is liberty?" exclaims the Turkish participant at the Mecca conference. "This is something that was withheld from us till we forgot it, and we were forbidden even to utter it until we became estranged from it." By Kawakibi's definition, liberty means that "man can choose what to say and do without obstruction and oppression." It includes the novel Western-inspired ideals of equal rights, accountability of rulers, and freedom of instruction, preaching, publishing, and research, along with the Islamic ideals of justice and the protection of religion, life, and honor. For Kawakibi, liberty is the very spirit of religion and the most precious thing for a man next to his life. Taking it from him results in despair, inaction, and lawlessness.

Second to liberty is the idea of modern science, the source of the material superiority of the West. It is presented at the Mecca conference by the Kurdish participant, a mathematician by profession. He laments the rejection of the exact and natural sciences by the Muslim tradition – to such an extent that those who found interest in them were dubbed heretics. As these sciences began to flourish in the West, they yielded prodigious material as well as spiritual fruits, "till they became like the sun, which no living being can live without." Kawakibi believed that Muslims needed the modern sciences not only to keep pace with the other nations in all matters, from education and politics to agriculture and industry. In line with the apologetic tone of Modernist reformers such as Abduh and Rida, he also argued that the scientific discoveries in astronomy, physics, and chemistry, and even "the principle of evolution established by the great savant Darwin," helped uncover the secrets of the Quran and prove the logical and moral superiority of the Muslim religion.

Two other ideas that betray Kawakibi's Western inspiration are those of social justice and solidarity. Both have deep roots in Islam, but with the development of the socialist and nationalist ideologies they have become identified with the West. At the Mecca conference, he therefore assigns the discussion of their merits to the English participant. According to him, Islamic social justice is enshrined in the duties of almsgiving and financial expiation, which, if fulfilled, will guarantee the distribution of wealth in society and cover public expenses. Today, however, claims the felicitous Englishman, it is rather the West that, largely thanks to the efforts of the socialist and nihilist movements, has eliminated poverty and promoted social legislation and economic equality.

In the same vein, Islam provides ample opportunity to forge social solidarity through the hajj pilgrimage and the Friday sermon. Yet, while the ulama and preachers have stayed away from public affairs and the common people have turned to attend to their own business, the Western nations have encouraged national public meetings and discussions. In terms that anticipate Benedict Anderson's imagined communities, the English participant specifies how Westerners have fixed times for socializing by instituting a weekly day of rest and holidays, allocated special places for speeches and processions in the city squares, parks, and clubs, and fostered nationalist feelings by spreading collective myths and heroic tales, erecting memorials, and publishing events and opinion articles in the newspapers.

The figure of the English participant also serves Kawakibi to demonstrate the basic affinity between his Salafi call and the Protestant Reformation. He thanks God that most of his community of converts in Liverpool hail from the evangelical Protestant denomination, rather than from the traditional Catholic one, a fact that inclines them to rely only on the Quran and Sunna. Moreover, Protestants are one of the two major groups of Westerners targeted by the missionary (*da'wa*) association he established, with affiliations in America and South Africa. "We place our hope in the Protestants because they turned their back to Catholicism out of their preference to rely only on the New Testament and the scriptures, to the exclusion of unfounded commentaries, exegeses and accretions." The other group targeted by the Islamic mission in the West is the atheists (*zanadiqa*), those who have despaired of Christianity and left religion altogether. Both groups, Kawakibi believed, were ready to accept the rational, liberal, and tolerant call of Islam.

AN ASSOCIATION FOR MUSLIM EDIFICATION

Identifying ignorance in general, and religious ignorance in particular, as the root cause of the malaise of the Muslims of his day leads Kawakibi in the final part of the Mecca conference to institutionalize it in the form of an imaginary body, *The Association for the Edification of God's Unifiers*. The draft of its regulations is entrusted to a preparatory committee consisting of "those among us who have acquired experience in scientific associations, or who have knowledge of the structures of statutory associations, especially the Western ones that are called academies." These are the English, Egyptian, and Indian participants, a composition that signals Kawakibi's admiration for the British model, along with the Turkish participant, who, he now is at pains to point out, comes from Kashgar in western China and not from the Ottoman Empire. Al-Sayyid al-Furati was the secretary of this committee too. The draft is carefully worked out, with attention to every detail, as it was certainly intended to be a model for such associations in the real world. It was then debated in three consecutive sessions of the conference, before its final promulgation in the last session, the twelfth.

The Association for the Edification of God's Unifiers was to follow what Kawakibi defines as the moderate Salafi orientation, which adheres to no existing school or sect of Islam. The qualifier moderate (*mu'tadil*) indicates that, unlike his previous references to the theological stand of the Wahhabis, here he has in mind a new form of Salafism, one that conciliates the model of the *salaf* with the achievements of the modern West. This designation thus establishes Kawakibi as one of the earliest self-conscious proponents of the Modernist Salafiyya and a major source of influence on its principal propagator after World War I, Rashid Rida. The association was to be a nonpolitical organization and associated with no government. The regulations specify the various bodies of the association, their membership, and functions. Its supreme authority, a general assembly of 100 members, was to convene once a year to elect in a free and secret ballot the executive and advisory bodies, supervise their actions, and chart their course. The center of the association was to remain in Mecca, with branches throughout the Muslim world. The expenses of the association were to be covered by two sources: its publications and donations by rulers and the wealthy.

As to its mission, the association was to work through the religious scholars to reform, regulate, and modernize traditional learning. This included the spread of literacy, encouraging the acquisition of useful professions and specialization, improving the methods of teaching of the religious sciences and of Arabic, and the unification and simplification of textbooks. Concomitantly, the association was to work with rulers in order to create a supervisory religious authority to prevent unauthorized teaching and preaching. Another task of the ulama was to direct the masses to respect the rights of the non-Muslims and treat them well. Finally, the association was entitled to sponsor various scientific expeditions and publications, ranging from moral books and pamphlets to a monthly journal in the main four Muslim languages: Arabic, Turkish, Persian, and Urdu.

Following the unanimous approval of the regulations by all participants in the Mecca conference, the chairman notes its decision to begin preparations for founding the association in Egypt or Kuwait – two territories under nominal Ottoman suzerainty but actually under British rule – and appointed the Egyptian luminary and al-Sayyid al-Furati to make all the necessary arrangements. A little farther on, in a passage apparently added shortly after Kawakibi's emigration, he says: "our association has chosen to establish its temporary center in Egypt, the land of science and freedom," in the hope that Khedive Abbas II would support it, "as he is the best young ruler raised on religious zeal and Arab fervor." Kawakibi promises to inform the participants about their progress and invites them to a farewell celebration, at which some secret matters were to be divulged and a new code distributed. He concludes with a poem he received from the absent Lebanese man of letters, which reads:

This is your means and there is no other / Strive for your revival, the best of nations
Without the community of God's unity / You will never find anything to unite you
Religious conduct is the best way / For all creatures, Arab and non-Arab
In it is life and your glory / Green black of the commandment and the holy

AN ARAB CALIPHATE

In the final sections of *The Mother of Cities*, Kawakibi raises two more issues that hitherto have been mentioned only in passing: Arabism and the Caliphate. Although their discussion is framed respectively as merely an appendix and an afterword to the conference, and is probably the last to be put into writing, these are indeed integral components of his Islamic reform. The Arab question appears as "decision no. 6" of the secret deliberations, held at the farewell meeting in Mecca, an allusion to the opposition that Kawakibi expected to meet on the part of the Ottoman Sultan. His views on the Caliphate are discussed in a letter that al-Sayyid al-Furati received two months after the conclusion of the conference from the Indian participant reporting on a conversation he had held with an unnamed distinguished Muslim amir. At the turn of the century, Indian Muslims were becoming the staunchest supporters of the Ottoman Caliphate, so Kawakibi's doctrine must be seen, at least partially, as a response to their concerns.

Decision no. 6 is the document that secured for Kawakibi pride of place in the pantheon of the precursors of Arab nationalism. For most of the twentieth century, it was regarded as the most important part of his teaching. It asserts that the Arabian Peninsula, its inhabitants, and the Arabs in general are the most suited to lead the regeneration of Islam. In line with the racial perceptions then in vogue, it further clarifies that other nations are also to contribute to the general goal of Islamic unity, each according to its distinctive merits: political and diplomatic affairs are assigned to the Ottoman Turks; civilizational matters are delegated to the Egyptians; military affairs are the province of a host of nations, from the Afghans and Caucasians in the east to Moroccans and Black Africans in the west; and scientific and economic affairs are to be left to the Iranians and Indians.

The special characteristics that make the Arabs the key to pan-Islamic, and "Eastern," unity are religious as well as national: the Arabian Peninsula is the provenance of Islam and its geographic center; it is also the most pure racially and the farthest off from foreigners. The Arabs of the Peninsula are the most ardent adherents of Islam, and the most knowledgeable about it, because it was revealed to them and because they have kept to the original Salafi faith; as Bedouin, they are also a noble and enduring race that sustains its solidarity and freedom and resists injustice. The Arabs in general are the speakers of the language of the Quran, which is the common language of all Muslims; they are also the first nation to practice equality, consultation, social cooperation, and humanism. They guided other nations on the initial path of Islam in the past and are the most suited to leading them today.

By contrast, the imaginary conversation reported by the Indian comrade, in which Kawakibi advances the complementary idea of a spiritual Caliphate, has been contested by Islamic reformers from his time to this day. When the Muslim amir insists on the return of the Caliphate to the Arabs, his Indian interlocutor ponders whether the established Ottoman state is not better situated to fortify Islam than the weak Arabs, "especially as the umma has been long accustomed to hear the title of 'service of the two Holy Places' (*khidmat al-haramain*) and more recently the title *khilafa* in relation to the Ottoman Sultan." The lofty Sultan, was the answer, may support and reinforce religion but he cannot conduct it, "because religion is one thing and government is another."

Kawakibi was well aware of the explosive nature of this statement, and the Indian comrade is accordingly made to react with total incomprehension. A quarter of a century later, after the abolition of the Caliphate by the Turkish parliament, the Azhari alim Ali Abd al-Raziq (1888–1966) would lose his scholarly title and public functions for adopting a similar position and questioning the necessity of an Islamic government. For Kawakibi, however, the secular principle of the separation of religion and politics was the solution to the fundamental dilemma that irritated him and his Salafi colleagues of the late Ottoman Empire, namely that the strongest Muslim state was also the bastion of the conservatives and a fierce opponent of Islamic reform. Combining his habitual historical insights with those of political philosophy, he argues that the Ottoman Sultans' respect for religion has been merely a facade, and that state interests by necessity always have superseded religion. All the more, considering that the Ottoman lands consisted of a multitude of diverse religions and denominations, while the Ottoman Sultans have never had any hesitation conniving with non-Muslims against rival Muslim dynasties when the need has arisen. This has been demonstrated in many cases, old and new. In the heyday of empire, Kawakibi remonstrates, Mehmet the Conqueror allowed Ferdinand and Isabella to persecute and eliminate the Muslim presence in Andalusia, Selim betrayed the Abbasid house after his conquest of the Arab lands, and Suleiman oppressed and humiliated the Iranian Shi'is. In the period of Ottoman decline, Mahmud II imposed European dress on the servants of state, and his successor Abdulmecid legalized usury and the consumption of alcohol, abolished Quranic punishments, and degraded the Prophet's progeny by undermining their organization, the *niqabat al-ashraf*, believing that such measures were essential for reforming the administration of the Empire.

Still, whether out of conviction or simply by sheer prudence, Kawakibi hews to the line he adopted at the onset of his career, and exonerates Abdulhamid II from such charges. The Indian amir expresses his hope that the present Sultan will support religion, and places the blame for his pretentions to the Caliphate on "sycophant imposter traitors" – another reference to Abu al-Huda al-Sayyadi and his ilk, "who attribute to the Sultan what he or any of his predecessors have never claimed for themselves." Through extravagant praise and a barrage of books and pamphlets, they invented false claims for the Ottomans' right to the Caliphate, such as a relation to the third Caliph Uthman or to the Prophet's tribe Quraysh, receiving the office from the Abbasids, a collective oath of allegiance to them, and their custodianship of the two Holy Places. Concomitantly, these imposters arrogate to themselves the highest mystical states and spiritual leadership, and invent genealogies replete with miracles and falsehoods that relate them to the government. Their efforts, the amir argues, "push and lead his highness the present Sultan to surrender established imperial rights for a fancied title of Caliphate bound by heavy restrictions and unfit for the circumstances of state, and thus expose him to agitation, dispossession and great danger."

Kawakibi's design for the Arab Caliphate draws instead on the religious model of the Catholic papacy and the political models of the federal systems of the United States and Germany, while on the procedural side it bears an affinity to the regulations of his *Association for the Edification of God's Unifiers*. It stipulates that an Arab Caliph from the Quraysh is to be instated in Mecca; like the Pope, his political authority will be confined to his immediate environment – the Hijaz – and attached to a local council; he will have no right to intervene in the political and administrative affairs of other Muslim countries, will command no military force, and will rely on a mixed Arab contingent to maintain order in the Hijaz. Beside the Caliph, a general Islamic council (*shura*) is to be formed, whose functions are likewise strictly limited to matters of general religious policy. Like the edification association, it will consist of 100 members representing all Muslim countries, and will convene once a year before the hajj in Mecca. Among its responsibilities are the election of the Caliph and renewal of his office every three years.

Kawakibi's plan to separate an Ottoman Sultanate from an Arab Caliphate was thus designed to reconcile the contradictory needs of a strong Muslim government and a radical Islamic reform. He assures the Indian Muslims and his readers at large that such a separation will actually enhance the prospects of unity. On the other hand, Kawakibi seeks to allay Western apprehensions that the Caliphate may become a political union and lead to religious wars. In his conception, spelled out from the very beginning of the Mecca conference, jihad meant making every effort for the sake of religion as well as for this world, rather than merely war against non-Muslims, whereas its rules forbid the use of coercion in religious matters. Moreover, from his point of view, the Arabs in particular testify to the friendly nature of Islam. Again ahead of most of his Modernist Salafi contemporaries, Kawakibi argues that the Arabs abandoned jihad seven centuries ago, that is, after the Crusade wars, and that at the time of writing they have distanced themselves from the Ottoman massacres of the Armenians. They are even ready to accept the rule of the colonial powers, he promises, seeing it as the will of God.

Kawakibi's inclination to the Arabs of the Peninsula, and especially his embrace of the secular principle of the separation of religion and politics, encountered fierce opposition from friend and foe alike. When these ideas first appeared in print in Egypt in 1899, authored under the pseudonym "free thinking Muslim," even Rida strongly objected. Subscribing to the Western ideal of progress, he pointed out that the Arab Bedouin represented merely an early, pre-civilizational, stage on the human ladder, whose apex was the civilization of Islam, and that Islamic unity must be based on the sharia and faith, rather than on tribal affiliation and language. As an avowed follower of Afghani and Abduh, Rida also advocated their form of pan-Islam, for which religion was an essential tool for the political unity of the umma in the face of the Western onslaught. The separation of religion and state was strongly denounced by Rida, who seems to have been unaware of the identity of the author, as a diabolic idea that only the enemies of Islam could pronounce in their wish to eliminate the rule of Islam from the face of the earth! Kawakibi's response to Rida and other critics was that Rida himself did not believe in the Ottoman Caliphate, and that to be part of the modern world the Muslims, more particularly the Arabs, must learn to rely on themselves rather than the government in correcting their religion and managing their worldly affairs.

Abd al-Rahman al-Kawakibi's scheme for the regeneration of the Muslim umma is then informed by two perspectives. On the religious side, he embraces the Wahhabis' call to follow the scriptures as these were understood and practiced by the *salaf*, though unlike them he seeks to set right the domains of jurisprudence and Sufism rather than supersede them. This bears a resemblance to the Protestant reformation, the Western model for a return to a pristine rational religion. On the political side, Kawakibi follows the Young Ottomans in adopting modern Western ideals such as liberty, science, socialism, and patriotism, while stressing the role of the Arabs in the formation of the Muslim umma. These two perspectives converge in a new sense of enlightened Salafi orientation that is geared to remold and modernize the Islamic principles of consultation, knowledge, justice, and solidarity.

The scope of the religious educational society Kawakibi envisaged to effect the Salafi reformation was certainly much broader than the local associations that sprang up in Syria and Egypt during his time. It is the primacy of the Arabs in the religious sphere and the creation of an Arab spiritual Caliphate at the side of the Ottoman worldly Sultanate, however, that constitute the special contribution of *The Mother of Cities* to the ongoing debate on Muslim regeneration and Islamic reform. Together, these ideas amount to a pan-Islamic program that constituted an alternative both to Abdulhamid's conservative plan, which Kawakibi attributed to the machinations of Abu al-Huda rather than the Sultan himself, and to the revolutionary intrigues of Afghani, which made Islam a mere political tool. Kawakibi's unique embrace of the secular principle of the separation of religion and politics was thus ultimately designed to chart a middle way that would give both politics and religion their due place in the overall regeneration of Islam.

6

AGAINST TYRANNY

A SCIENTIFIC INQUIRY

The Nature of Tyranny and the Injuries of Enslavement originated in a series of articles that Kawakibi began to publish anonymously soon after his emigration to Egypt. The first article is dated 17 March 1899. They appeared in the influential paper *al-Muayyad* of Shaykh Ali Yusuf, who was close to Khedive Abbas Hilmi as well as to the reformists. Although the ideas contained in these articles must have been conceived already in Aleppo, Kawakibi apparently refrained from committing them to writing so long as he was within reach of the Ottoman authorities. None of his colleagues in Aleppo knew about them and they expressed surprise at the news of their appearance in Egypt. In view of the enthusiastic reception of his articles among the intellectual circles in Egypt, Kawakibi decided to expand them into a book, on which he continued to work even after publication and until his last day. *The Nature of Tyranny* too appeared under the signature *al-Rahhala K* and was dedicated to the Arab youth. To the front matter of the second printing Kawakibi added his proud identification as an Arab Muslim. Fortunately, his son Kazim managed to rescue the last copy his father was working on from the Ottoman agents who came to seize his papers upon his death. It remained in the custody of Rashid Rida until he returned it to the family when visiting Syria in 1920. The manuscript was in very bad shape, and it took Kawakibi's other son As'ad years to rehabilitate it. A new edition with additions and emendations, which amounted to almost a third of the original work, was finally published in 1957 by his grandson Dr. Abd al-Rahman al-Kawakibi.

Observers did not fail to notice already in Kawakibi's day that *The Nature of Tyranny* was indebted to political thinkers of the European Enlightenment such as Montesquieu and Rousseau. Kawakibi himself was the first to admit, in the very first lines of the book, that it contained "what he studied by himself and what he took from others." Sylvia Haim has suggested as its specific source of inspiration the 1777 book *Della Tirannide* (On Tyranny) by the Italian author Vittorio Alfieri, who is mentioned once toward the end of the work. Kawakibi could have learned about it from his friends in the Italian community of Aleppo, or more plausibly from the Turkish translation by the Young Turk writer and activist Abdallah Jevdet, which appeared in 1898, shortly before he left for Egypt. Still, there is no reason to doubt Kawakibi's assertion, to which his earliest formulations in *al-Shahba* and *al-I'tidal* and his mature thought in *Umm al-Qura* are plain evidence, that it was thirty years of inquiry into the social and political problems of the Muslims, and of the East at large, that made him realize that their root cause was despotic government, and that the remedy must begin with the formation of a constitutional government.

The Nature of Tyranny is framed as a scientific inquiry in the field of political philosophy. It consists of a preamble on the discipline of politics together with some definitions of tyranny, followed by eight chapters that analyze the relation of the absolutist mode of government with various aspects of life, from religion and ethics to economy and society. Each chapter discusses this relation in theory and in its actuality in the Muslim world. The book concludes with a series of questions for further reflection under the rubric of the escape from tyranny. Kawakibi asserts in the introduction that his study does not target any specific government, and nowhere in the work does he mention Abdulhamid II. It has been generally assumed, by contemporary and later generations of readers and scholars, that it was nonetheless the Sultan whom he saw before him. Yet, Kawakibi's career, in which he was time and again saved by the Palace from the iniquities of the local administration, makes us take more seriously his claim that it was tyranny as a system rather than the person of the Sultan that he targeted. The work as a whole marks the return of his focus to the realm of politics, his principal concern since the early days of journalistic enterprise.

Like *The Mother of Cities*, the literary form of *The Nature of Tyranny* is part of its message, and it likewise serves Kawakibi in a number of ways. To begin with, a scientific study of the absolutist government is designed to expose its evils, but also to demonstrate the importance of critical thinking, which is one of the basic conditions for its replacement by a liberal democratic form of government. Next, the very undertaking of such an investigation signifies the responsibility that Muslims must shoulder if they are to solve the malaise of their polity and society, rather than blame their plight on others or on fate. Finally, by enlisting the authority of Western science and philosophy, Kawakibi seeks not only to enhance the validity of his conclusions, but also to provide the new class of religious intellectuals to which he belonged with a practical guide to the employment of science in general, and the Enlightenment ideas of liberty, reason, unity, and progress in particular, in the service of the reform of Islam. In this context, he makes a crucial distinction between the appropriation of useful Western ideas and plain imitation of its materialist hedonist culture.

DEFINING TYRANNY

Kawakibi begins his study in his usual manner with a brief survey of the evolution of the discipline of politics as a universal science and philosophy that concerns the Western and the Muslim nations alike. According to him, it started with occasional remarks in the history, ethics and law books of antiquity, especially those of Republican Rome, and continued with references in the works of medieval Muslim scholars such as the theologian Ghazzali, the poet Mutanabbi, and the historian Ibn Khaldun. It was, however, the modern Europeans, Kawakibi points out to his Muslim readers, who established it as an independent field; they greatly expanded its scope and created its various branches, from foreign and internal affairs to administrative, economic, and legal issues. In the course of the nineteenth century, the Muslims, particularly the Turks but also the Arabs, followed in their footsteps and wrote about political matters in books and more especially the press. Yet few of them, he claims, dared to tackle the most important political issue of all, namely tyrannical government.

For Kawakibi, tyranny is the antithesis of politics. If politics is the prudent conduct of public affairs, tyranny is their capricious conduct. By his definition, tyranny in general means one's reliance on one's own opinion when consultation is required. It may apply to religious leaders, family heads, and guild masters, but it is especially used in the case of governments, the most powerful factor in rendering human beings the most miserable creatures on earth! According to political science definitions, Kawakibi continues, tyranny is the property of the absolutist government, which is bound neither by law, whether the sharia or any other system, nor by the will of the people. Tyrannical power may be exercised by an individual, who usually assumes power by force or through inheritance, a collectivity, or even a corrupt constitutional government, so long as these are not accountable for their deeds. Moreover, history shows that even responsible civilized governments are prone to degenerate into tyranny once their supervision by their people slackens. The fate of the Caliphs Uthman and Ali in early Islam and the Panama and Dreyfus affairs in contemporary France are cases in point. As against these, Kawakibi notes two exceptions: one is the current English government, thanks to the alertness of the English people; the other is the Bedouin governments, particularly those of the Arabian Peninsula, since the tribes could always slip away into the desert once their freedom was in jeopardy. As we have seen in *The Mother of Cities*, these were respectively the modern government he most admired and the Muslim society he believed was most suitable to accommodate it.

In the second edition of *The Nature of Tyranny*, Kawakibi adds, perhaps in reflection of his travels in colonial Asia and Africa, a discussion of the evils of militarism. Every government, he maintains, is prone to lapse into tyranny when left unchecked by the use of two principal means: the ignorance of the people and military service. The civilized nations have basically freed themselves from ignorance, but instead have become afflicted with general compulsory conscription, which makes them even more miserable than the ignorant nations. Army service corrupts morals, breeds wickedness, blind obedience, dependence, and inactivity, and overburdens the nation's resources. Along with ignorance, militarism is thus the mainstay of both indigenous tyrants and the European colonial states.

THE POLITICO-RELIGIOUS NEXUS

The first issue to be examined in *The Nature of Tyranny* on the basis of these preliminary considerations is the relation between tyranny and religion. Kawakibi notes that in European political science political tyranny is regarded as the product of religious tyranny or as closely connected to it. This is true in the case of primitive religions and of the historical parts of the Old and the New Testament, he argues, but totally wrong with regard to the doctrinaire parts of the Jewish and Christian scriptures, and to the Quran in its entirety. The political scientists might be excused for their mistake, however, on two grounds. One is their inability to comprehend the secrets of the Quran, the other is the present state of the Muslims, which seems to confirm their views. The latter ground gives Kawakibi the opportunity to lend scientific authority to his critique of the Muslim polity and society of his day; the former reemphasizes the role of religion as the cornerstone of authentic reform and confirms the need for religious thinkers like himself to chart the way.

Scholars further claim, according to Kawakibi, that all religions, polytheist as well as monotheist, inculcate in their believers fear of an incomprehensible mighty entity, which threatens man with terrifying afflictions in this world and unutterable punishment in the next. They then open the door to salvation through a human screen (*hijab*), namely the men of religion, who while posing as lofty persons do not shy away from demanding excessive reverence along with full payment for their services. The absolutist rulers erect their systems on the same foundations, maintains Kawakibi. They sow awe in the hearts of the people by elevating their own person and resort to coercion and plunder to humiliate and force them into submission and servitude. This similarity causes the common people to confound Almighty God with the oppressive tyrant, and to regard them as equal in their status and attributes, therefore entitled to the same boundless reverence. Exploiting the situation, past tyrants claimed some form or other of divinity for themselves, and to this day they continue to promote religion and men of religion to help them oppress their subjects.

The conclusion that Muslim scholars should draw from this discussion is that political tyranny and religious tyranny indeed go hand in hand, and that therefore religious reform is the most effective way to political reform. The first to attempt this path, in Kawakibi's narrative construction, were the ancient Greek savants, who by imagining multiple gods, each charged with a specific function, persuaded their kings to likewise share in their political power. This led to the creation of the republics of Athens and Sparta, and later Rome. But this path ultimately failed as it generated a multiplicity of small tyrants in place of the few big ones, and of religious imposters who were happy to serve them. After all, in Islam paganism is by definition null and void. The Torah and the Gospel then introduced the belief in one God but, according to Muslim doctrine, were later corrupted: the former by the Israelite kings, and the latter by the Epistles of Paul and the clergy, which came to be seen as the infallible deputy of God. The Protestants, who called for reform based on a return to the original commandments of the Gospel, Kawakibi points out, rejected such claims.

Finally, Islam arrived on the scene to destroy all manifestations of associating others with God (*shirk*) and to enhance freedom through a moderate government based on a combination of democracy and aristocracy. The rightly guided Caliphs, Kawakibi maintains, fully realized the meanings of the Quran and implemented them with justice and equality, social solidarity, and economic cooperation. Most importantly, contrary to the tyrannical mode of government, their rule was based on the principle of consultation. Citing Quranic verses, which enjoin it, Kawakibi can thus declare that Islamism (*islamiyya*) – the idealized and objectified Islam of the *salaf* – was based on the foundations of popular democratic administration and aristocratic consultation among the elite (*ashraf*).

Lamentably, however, as in the Jewish and Christian cases, Islam too was corrupted in the course of time. Reiterating his analysis of the malady of the Muslim community in his imaginary conference at *Umm al-Qura* – asceticism, visiting saints' tombs, the false Caliphate and their like – Kawakibi argues that such unlawful innovations invariably lead to tyranny. As against them he poses the miracle of the Quran, which for him and the early Salafis in general was the clearest and incorruptible manifestation of God's wisdom, but also an ever-renewing guide for the establishment of good government.

KNOWLEDGE AND PUBLIC SERVICE

Once the fault line between "true" Islam and tyranny has been established, Kawakibi proceeds, in line with the title of his book, to examine the absolutist rationale and its political, social, and psychological damages. First in his sequence is the question of knowledge (*'ilm*), the principal precondition for effective participation in the political arena. The tyrant, says Kawakibi, knows very well that his rule depends on his subjects' stupefaction and ignorance. He has no problem with the religious sciences that focus on the other world, or with the study of foreign languages, but he is terrified by the sciences of this life – speculative wisdom, rational philosophy, the rights of nations, civil politics, history, and oratory, which broaden the mind and teach men about themselves and about their rights and how to demand, attain, and protect them. The tyrant detests knowledge, because of these consequences, and in itself, as something that is more powerful than the government.

In short, between tyranny and science rages an everlasting war; the ulama – the people of religion but also the people of science – strive to spread knowledge, while the tyrant makes every effort to extinguish its light. This is a battle for the minds of the masses, Kawakibi maintains, which when in a state of ignorance are fearful and submissive, but once enlightened speak up and act. Undoubtedly on the basis of his own experience under the Hamidian regime, he avers that ignorant people dread their ruler and applaud him even though he oppresses them and plunders their property. He further predicts that, once ignorance is removed, the tyrant of necessity will transform into a just and loyal president who takes care of his people, before whom he is accountable. Indeed, in Kawakibi's view, the ruler himself would be the first to benefit from such a change of system, since he would no longer regard his subjects as well as his closest servants as enemies to be feared lest they depose him or take his life.

But for the time being, as Kawakibi knew all too well, the men of knowledge were persecuted, and the fortunate among them in his eyes were those who, like himself, managed to flee. The prophets and great ulama, says Kawakibi with reference to a famous hadith often cited by the Salafis, wandered in the world and died, strangers away from home. Islam, he later added, was the first religion to foster knowledge, and the first word in the Quran, in Angel Gabriel's revelation to Muhammad, was the order to read. The forefathers (*al-salaf al-awwal*) spread literacy among all Muslims and through them to the other nations until tyranny arrived and drew the umma back to ignorance.

Closely connected to knowledge is the question of honor (*majd*), which Kawakibi regards as the main drive for political action. Honor, he frankly admits, is a natural aspiration and a source of great satisfaction; for the free person, it is more important than life itself. Rather than an egoistic feeling, however, for him it derives from service to the community, in the way of

God and religion in Eastern terms and for the sake of humanity or the nation in Western terms. Honor entails, in ascending order, money donation, spreading of useful knowledge, and self-sacrifice, which under the absolutist government means resistance to oppression. The tyrannical system, by contrast, encourages vain boasting (*tamajjud*), a term that Kawakibi attaches to the ruler's favorites, assistants, and the notables, the recipients of his empty titles and awards. These are small tyrants, who thrive under the wing of the great tyrant. They present themselves as independent, but in reality they must endure constant insults and humiliation. Through them the tyrant misleads his subjects to believe that his futile wars are waged for the glory of religion and that his squandering of public funds is designed to protect the dignity of the community.

Reflecting on, and justifying, his work in the provincial administration of Ottoman Aleppo and his close connections with the notable class of the city, Kawakibi maintains that, along with these weak and mean servants, the tyrant also seeks to promote and use the abilities of intelligent and trustworthy persons whom he believes can be easily corrupted. Dismayed by their honesty, he maltreats them or expels them altogether. Citing the authority of scientific research, Kawakibi claims that this group, to which he himself belonged, "which had tasted the sweetness of government honor and of work in the service of the umma and the glory of nobility but was then struck on its hand only because it is trustful, is the group that becomes galvanized by hatred of tyranny and calls for reform." Similarly, while most of the notable families are condescending and oppressive, it happens that some of their more educated and perceptive offspring make use of the confidence and courage that their social standing and aristocratic upbringing have instilled in them to stand up to the mighty ones in the service of the fatherland and its people. Hinting at his own aspirations, Kawakibi adds that the most exceptional among these, who combine noble descent and personal talent, are the best suited to lead the nation to success.

SOCIALISM AND DEMOCRACY

After the preconditions and impulses for public action, Kawakibi turns his attention to the economic and ethical foundations of society and to the ways in which tyranny affects them. Again, both derive from the Quran and the practice of the early Muslim community, but are also made to accord with the loftiest ideals of modern Western civilization. Kawakibi's definition of the economic order as a common cooperative way of life (*ishtirak*), and his endeavors for the poorer classes of Aleppo, mark the dominance of socialist notions in his thought in this domain. In the second addition of *The Nature of Tyranny*, he further stresses that the poor do not want the assistance and mercy of the rich, but justice, which entails the distribution of wealth. Islam provides for justice, Kawakibi argues, by several means: the alms tax (*zakah*) and tithes, the income of which must be divided between public expenses and needy persons; public ownership (*milk*) of agricultural lands, the fruits of which belong to its cultivators; encouraging people to work for their living; and entrusting the government to take charge of all these, "as most Socialist associations demand today." On the other hand, financing private and public projects is allowed in Islam as long as it is not based on interest, exploitation, and hoarding.

In the tyrannical government, by contrast, it is easy to amass fortunes by stealing from the public treasury or by transgressing the rights of the common people. Any faithless and shameless person, as Kawakibi's bitter experience with the governor Jamil Pasha and Sheikh Abu al-Huda allowed him to claim, might grow rich by joining the system or by trading in religion, lending money, and running immoral entertainment houses. As in the case of the tyrant at the top of the pyramid, however, the wealthy themselves cannot enjoy their property because, on the one hand, they have to squander their fortunes in ostentatious ways to create awe in the hearts of those below them, while, on the other, they are forced to conceal it and pretend to be poor before their covetous superiors. Such an economic system could have worked in the past, Kawakibi reasons, but at present the public treasury has become a crucial tool for the independence of the country, so nations that lack it lose all standing in human society.

The mainstay of public morality is the Quranic commandment to forbid the wrong (*al-nahi 'an al-munkar*), which Kawakibi parallels to the freedom of speech in democracy. Forbidding the wrong, and any kind of criticism, he writes, is anathema to tyranny, which strives to weaken and corrupt man's natural disposition and turn him against his nation, fatherland, family, and friends. People under such a system are nothing but prisoners in his eyes. Like the beasts, they are preoccupied with survival and have no interest in intellectual or social life. The masses hardly distinguish good from bad, and are dazzled by pomp and panoply into blind submission to the ruler. Using a well-known Sufi simile to drive home a different lesson, Kawakibi likens them to insects that are attracted to fire and resist anyone who tries to save them from destruction. More perplexing still, as they lack the courage to stand up to the iniquitous ruler, they turn their wrath unjustly against the weak or foreigners, or simply against their wives. In the tyrannical system, there is thus little room for forbidding the wrong, by advice or by reproach. Only hypocrites and sycophants would take to preaching and guidance under such conditions and few would care to heed them.

As against this, in the free government, every person has the right to criticize others, including those in power, without fear, and thus make a difference. Kawakibi leaves no doubt as to his admiration for the Western democratic system. The free nations, he says, have instituted freedom of speech, writing, and publication, on the understanding that this is the only way to prevent rulers from strangling freedom. On this basis, they also created parliaments to control and review public administration. As in the economic domain, and eventually in the universe at large, the secret of success of the civilized nations lies in the principle of *ishtirak*, which in the political domain, according to Kawakibi's aristocratic notions, is translated into popular participation under the guidance of a committed elect.

But criticism can also be directed at democracy, when it is deprived of its divine origins. The humanist confidence in man's intellect, the equation between religion and tyranny, the spread of science (through the agency of the Arabs), and the common bond of national patriotism, Kawakibi writes, led Westerners to a false conception of freedom. This has had dire consequences, as unrestrained leaders have driven their peoples to moral deprivation and dreadful crimes that no ruler in the East would allow. The Western philosophers of the Enlightenment, who heralded the French Revolution, were, however, of a different ilk. They followed in the footsteps of the prophets, the first to deliver people from tyrannical rule, and like them enlightened the people in the principles of reason and free choice, as well as in the duties of humanity and morality. They did not proclaim a new religion nor attack religion as such; instead, they renewed and revived their religion and patched up the rifts of their time. Easterners, Kawakibi maintains, whether Buddhists, Muslims, Christians, or Jews, are today in need of such philosophers to return their religions to their sources.

Tyranny, by contrast, encourages the ritualistic aspect of religion but destroys its more important ethical aspect. In classical

Muslim doctrine, it is moral education (*tarbiya*) that determines whether man is to realize his natural disposition for the good or for the bad. Kawakibi further stresses that such education must consist of both knowledge and practice (*'ilm wa-'amal*). In the enslaved nations, he claims, no one knows what education is and how it should be practiced. Tyranny teaches people to use such devices as deceit and trickery, hypocrisy and self-effacement, and thus generates slaves, with no control of their own selves and no motivation to educate their children. Prisoners know only of carnal pleasures and are deprived of all spiritual delights, from knowledge and honor to wellbeing and free opinion.

TOWARD PROGRESS

Progress is Kawakibi's master word for all the positive ideals that oppose the ills of tyranny. Subscribing to the nineteenth-century optimistic view of the march forward, for him this is the cornerstone as well as the principal instrument for personal empowerment, national solidarity, and human fraternity. It is also in full accord with the religio-ethical imperative of ordaining the good and forbidding the wrong, the essence of Islamism. Progress, Kawakibi maintains, is the movement of life. A nation in which the signs of progress are dominant is a living nation, while its opposite is a dead one. The tyrannical government deflects man's natural striving to advance, turning the march of progress into decline and growth into annihilation. Its effects are such that if its subjects are urged to elevate themselves they become resentful and pained, and if forced into freedom they complain and feel at loss. Tyranny is like a leech, sucking the blood of the nation and leaving it dead.

On the individual level, the prisoners of tyranny live a static life and are deprived of their senses and mores. They are the last to be blamed, however, since there is nobody to guide them on a different path. This is the task that Kawakibi seeks to assume for himself and for the progressive religious intellectual class he represents. In the second edition of *The Nature of Tyranny*, he mentions that some Western sociologists, apparently referring to the Positivists, argue that religion obstructs personal and collective progress, and that religion and reason contradict each other. This view is undoubtedly true in the case of a superstitious religion, like Christianity with its belief in the Trinity, he retorts. Islam, however – that of the Quran, not as practiced by most Muslims today – is built on reason and its commands are the most beneficial for humanity. Turning directly to the people, Kawakibi urges them to become conscious of their backwardness and inaction, to stop complaining and humbling themselves before the mighty ones, to obey only God and to have solidarity with one another. Addressing more specifically the Muslims, Kawakibi reminds them that oppression (*zulm*) is the second grossest wrong after disbelief, and that it is incumbent on each and every one of them, as the hadith ordains, to remove it from themselves and from others by hand, tongue, or heart.

On the national level, unlike in *The Mother of Cities*, Kawakibi directs his call initially to the non-Muslim Arabs, more particularly the Christian proponents of the *nahda*, who were "the first to tread the path of enlightenment in this region." Alluding to the communal riots that racked the Ottoman cities during the era of the later Tanzimat, Kawakibi urges the Christians to leave the affronts of the past behind them and pursue the unity of the fatherland. The examples he adduces are those of the Habsburg Empire and the United States, in which national unity and political solidarity have been established despite their religious diversity. Placing the blame for instigating communal hatred on the Western powers, Kawakibi urges his compatriots: "let us manage our own affairs in mutual understanding and fraternity," and reiterating his call to separate religion from politics in the face of Ottoman tyranny he adds: "let us manage our life in this world, and leave the religions to take care of the next world." The two aspects are combined in his motto "long live the nation, long live the fatherland, and long live the free and noble." The Westerner, Kawakibi warns his Christian compatriots and Easterners in general, has become a materialist whose religion is profit. His fraternity with the local Christians is nothing but deceit; however long he may live in the East, he always remains the oppressive colonialist and exploitative tradesman.

On the level of humanity at large, Kawakibi pins his hopes on the younger generation, to whom his book is dedicated. Warning against religious division and ignorance, he wishes them to be raised, unlike their fathers, as free people aware of their value, and to attain fame by noble intentions and great achievements. Each man should be independent in his personal conduct, ready to sacrifice for his nation and fatherland, and a friend to his fellow humans. Contrary to the accepted orthodox view, in the second edition of *The Nature of Tyranny* Kawakibi attributes the ascent of the West to some momentous developments that took place in the West itself: the formation of big nations, firepower, discoveries in chemistry and mechanics, coal, the development of a spirit of initiative, and the establishment of large financial companies. To deliver itself from external Western dominance, however, the East must first break its own internal chains of tyranny.

To this day, Kawakibi continues, no nation has attained the utmost degree of humanity, since none has been governed by public assent without any vestige of tyranny. Some governments approximated this ideal in the past, among them, in this order and mixture, the second Roman Empire, the rightly guided Caliphate, Nur al-Din Zangi, who fought the Crusades, and Peter the Great, founder of modern Russia. Contemporary governments that are close to it include Belgium, Switzerland, the United States, and Japan, which posed a firm barrier against tyranny and entrusted legislation to the people. It is only in such an ambience, Kawakibi believes, that the loftiest mode of progress, spiritual progress, can move man to set his nation, freedom, honor, and family before himself, and expand his feelings to include all humankind and the whole earth.

Having demonstrated the evil nature of tyranny and its grave harm to man and society, Kawakibi concludes his study with a discussion of the ways to eliminate it. He first suggests a general framework of four historical-existential modes of government: the state of nature in which experience and force are decisive, the nomadic free association, sedentary oppressive rule, and the affluent urbanized West. These are divided into two pairs, so that the Bedouin are paralleled to the free West, while sedentary life is as oppressive as the state of nature. Settling the form of government, Kawakibi maintains, has always been the greatest problem in human society, and the greatest battleground of philosophers and common people alike. Modern Western people, however, have managed to establish a number of fundamental principles that are approved by both reason and experience, but are still unknown in the East. On their basis, he poses twenty-five research questions, which are designed to set the agenda for political reform. These refer to the nature of the nation and the government, their mutual rights and duties, the source of sovereignty, the government's accountability, the rule of law, security, justice, and religion, separation of powers, and economic and scientific progress. A nation that succumbs to tyranny, Kawakibi concludes, does not deserve freedom, though the struggle against such government entails preparation and gradation, rather than rash violent action. The failures of tyranny facilitated the Western colonial enterprise, bringing upon the people of the East humiliation and subjugation; the struggle for freedom against the internal and external oppressors will regain their glory.

Abd al-Rahman al-Kawakibi's study of the effects of tyranny is one of the earliest essays in modern Arab Islamic political thought. It is also one of the sharpest indictments of the Hamidian regime, though of the system rather than the Sultan himself. Much more than *The Mother of Cities*, *The nature of Tyranny* draws on Western ideas of good government, with particular attention to the English model, albeit without ever relinquishing the Islamic precedents. With an eye to the Protestant Reformation, Kawakibi reiterates his sharp denunciation of the contemporary men of religion for their support of tyrannical rule in contravention of what he and fellow reformers saw as the original Islamic precepts of liberty and consultation. In the spirit of the Enlightenment and of the Arab *nahda*, he next stresses the importance of knowledge and science and the role of social and political activism in the struggle against tyranny. Ahead of most other Salafis of his day, he finally embraces the nineteenth-century economic teachings of the socialist movement, and the political form of democracy, though both remain guided by religion and led by the intellectual and political elite. Subsumed under the general idea of progress, which Kawakibi equates with movement and indeed with life itself, these advanced ideologies are his keys to personal empowerment, a supra-religious Arab national unity, and humanity's fraternity, the ideals that placed him at the forefront of the religious and political reformers of his time.

7

IN THE EYES OF POSTERITY

A MIDDLE-CLASS FAMILY

Abd al-Rahman al-Kawakibi's premature death in Egypt left his family in dire emotional and financial straits. His wife Fatima, who was preparing to join him in Cairo, refused to believe he was gone. The eldest son Kazim, who had accompanied him, returned to Aleppo after he had been pardoned and promised an appropriate position, but this failed to materialize. Following the Young Turk revolution of 1908, he applied for a license to launch a newspaper in Aleppo, but this initiative too bore no fruit. The next two brothers, As'ad and Rashid, were still studying at that time at the military school of medicine in Istanbul, and after graduation were assigned to different fronts in the Yemen, the Caucasus, and Libya. During World War I, As'ad was taken prisoner by the British, while the fourth brother, Ahmad Nu'man, who meanwhile had enrolled for pharmacy studies in Damascus, was sent to the Sinai front. The rest of the family suffered from the famine that hit Syria during the final years of the war, and had to rely on the youngest son, Fadil, who received a minor post in the railway company in Hama. The family's circumstances improved only after the sons serving in the army heard about their plight and arranged to transfer part of their officer rations to their mother. As'ad went on to join Faysal's Arab army and took part in the battle of Maysalun in July 1920, following which Syria succumbed to the French.

In the course of the twentieth century, the Kawakibis were able to recover partly, but never returned to their notable status. The last of the family to hold a high religious position was Abd al-Rahman's brother, Mas'ud, who, in the wake of the Young Turk revolution and the subsequent death of Abu al-Huda al-Sayyadi in 1909, was appointed *naqib al-ashraf* of Aleppo. He was dismissed from office by Jamal Pasha, the notorious military governor of Syria during World War I, after he refused to sign a *fatwa* that declared the leader of the Arab revolt, Sharif Hussein, a traitor. Mas'ud was reinstated by King Faysal after the formation of the Arab government in Damascus in 1918 but resigned following the French occupation of Syria two years later. The French authorities passed over his nephew As'ad, who had fought against them in Maysalun, and awarded the position to Sheikh Abd al-Razzaq al-Sayyadi (d. 1939), a half-brother of Abd al-Rahman al-Kawakibi's archenemy, Abu al-Huda.

Moreover, while the leading notable families of Aleppo – the Jabiris, the Qudsis, and their like – went on to consolidate their power under the French Mandate and played a conspicuous role in the democratic experiment after independence, the Kawakibi family settled for a more modest middle-class life, staying away from both politics and religion. Of Abd al-Rahman's sons, As'ad was a physician in Aleppo's health department, whereas his brother Rashid was a hospital director. Ahmad Nu'man operated a pharmacy and Fadil worked in agriculture. The most prominent representative of the grandsons' generation was his namesake, Dr. Abd al-Rahman al-Kawakibi, who gained his doctorate in 1951 from the Sorbonne. His dissertation dealt with social justice in Islam, a much discussed topic among the Muslim Brothers at the time, and included a chapter on his grandfather.

Another grandson, his biographer Sa'd Zaghlul al-Kawakibi, was a well-known figure in the city, a lawyer, judge, and president of the archeological society of Aleppo.

To this day, an acute sense of humiliation and abandonment permeates the public utterances of Abd al-Rahman al-Kawakibi's family. Sa'd Zaghlul, although obviously refraining from mentioning the Ba'th regime, was bitter at the indifference of successive Syrian governments to the legacy of his grandfather, and at their failure to bring his remains back home to Aleppo or to erect a statue to commemorate him. He also lamented the destruction of the Kawakibi *madrasa* and house after they had been transferred to the *awqaf* ministry, and complained of the many mistakes that appeared in new printings of Abd al-Rahman's books. As against this, Sa'd Zaghlul praised the sincere efforts exerted by the Egyptian Oriental Union Society to transfer his grandfather's remains to a respectable cemetery in the 1930s, and President Nasser's order to arrange a festival in his honor in the time of the United Arab Republic in the late 1950s. More recently, a granddaughter of Abd al-Rahman, Dahi, in an interview with the daily *al-Ahram* lauded the Egyptian government for its efforts to save the tomb that was once again in danger and for building a cultural center named after Kawakibi in front of it. The destruction of Aleppo in the civil war that has been raging in Syria since 2011 renders all hopes to perpetuate such gestures at home impracticable.

A MIXED LEGACY

Once the full import of Kawakibi's books became apparent to the Ottoman authorities, they were quick to put them on the proscribed list. Two booksellers from Beirut were sentenced to three years in prison with hard labor after a copy of *The Mother of Cities* was found in their shop. This did not prevent new prints of Kawakibi's works from appearing posthumously in Egypt and circulating in other Arab countries. In 1907, *The Nature of Tyranny* was translated into Persian by a disciple of the renowned Ayatollah Mirza Hussein Naini, one of the scholars who inspired Iran's constitutional revolution of 1906. Naini's censure of the conservative clerics who backed Qajar despotism led one Arab scholar to refer to him as "the Shi'a Kawakibi."

A constant stream of reprints of both Kawakibi's works continued to be published after the demise of the Ottoman Empire and the formation of the Arab state system at the end of World War I, and it has not ceased to this day. The only substantial new edition was that of *The Nature of Tyranny* completed by Dr. Abd al-Rahman al-Kawakibi in 1957, while two comprehensive collections of Kawakibi's oeuvre (*al-a'mal al-kamila*) were prepared and annotated respectively by the Egyptian Islamic scholar Muhammad Imara in 1976 and the Syrian intellectual Muhammad Jamal al-Tahhan in 1995. Several reprints of the Persian translation of *The Nature of Tyranny* have also appeared in Tehran, and in 1950 the book for the first time was translated into Urdu. Outside the Muslim world, the same book was translated into Russian in 1964, but to this day to the best of my knowledge no full translation of any of Kawakibi's works has come out in English or any other Western European language. A Hebrew translation of *The Mother of Cities*, the first translation of this work in any language, appeared this year (2015) in the Crescent Series that I edit, the aim of which is to make major Islamic works available to the Israeli public.

While in Western scholarship Kawakibi's works have been relatively neglected, in the Arab world they have drawn considerable attention and comment ever since they were published in 1900. However, the interpretation of his thought has undergone marked shifts as it has been appropriated, and at times misappropriated, by the diverse ideological formations vying for dominance in the Arab arena. Generally speaking, in the course of the past century, the various readings of Kawakibi have moved between the two major perspectives around which his thought revolved: Arab nationalism and Islamic reform. The shift of emphasis between them took place in the 1970s in the wake of the decline of pan-Arabism and the concomitant resurgence of Islam. Since the 1990s, there have also been attempts by some Arab intellectuals to evoke Kawakibi's legacy in their struggle for freedom and democracy.

In the first half of the twentieth century, throughout the national struggle against colonial rule, the religious aspect of Kawakibi's thought was relegated to the background, while the role he filled in the Arab cultural renaissance (*nahda*) and his pioneering effort in the formulation of the idea of Arabism were emphasized. His influence was marked on such early exponents of Arab nationalism as the Salafis Rashid Rida and Muhibb al-Din al-Khatib, the journalist and educator Muhammad Kurd Ali, and the Islamic nationalist Shakib Arslan. Expositions of his ideas at that time appeared mostly in the form of journal articles authored by his friends and acquaintances in the intellectual circles of his native city Aleppo and his place of exile Cairo. These were the authors who have also provided us with the bulk of our information on his life and career. In the Muslim Brothers Society, the first populist Islamic movement in the Arab world, the epistles of the founder, Hasan al-Banna, seem to have largely superseded highly stylized and sophisticated expositions such as Kawakibi's. Still, Banna's depiction of his movement as a preaching (*da'wa*) organization materialized Kawakibi's scheme for an association for the edification of the Muslim on a mass scale.

The interest in his teachings reached its peak in the 1950s and 1960s, the heyday of pan-Arabism, and more especially during the short-lived union of Syria and Egypt in the United Arab Republic

(UAR) in 1958–61. This period witnessed the proliferation of books that depicted Kawakibi as a great champion of the Arab nationalist cause, stressing his assertions about the Arabs' lofty virtues and values. These were harnessed to Nasser's pan-Arab ideology and the central role the Egyptian president envisaged for the Arabs as leaders of the Muslim world. Some of the authors further referred to Kawakibi's revolutionary aura implicit in his courageous condemnation of the despotic Ottoman regime, and to his support of socialism, two other major components in the official ideology of Nasserism as well as of the Ba'th party in Syria and Iraq. Many of the secular writers of this period were likewise sympathetic to his insistence on the separation of religion from politics.

While Kawakibi's advocacy of religious reform has never been entirely absent from the expositions of his thought, with the Islamic revival of the 1970s, this element has come to the fore. The change is demonstrated, for example, in the two otherwisc identical editions of his *Complete Works* by Imara: the second edition of 1984 appeared with an additional subtitle – *The Martyr of Freedom and Renewer of Islam*. Kawakibi, now habitually referred to as Imam al-Kawakibi, has never been principal reading in Islamist circles, but his work is appreciated for the reformist principles it laid down for the contemporary revival of Islam. Moreover, many authors have come to rely on his denunciation of the tyrannical government and its collaborative men of religion as support for their struggle against oppressive secular Arab rulers and the official religious establishments that legitimize them. Other Islamic writers and preachers, however, express serious reservations about Kawakibi's acrimonious critique of the now rehabilitated Islamically based Ottoman state, and especially the secular principle of the separation of religion and state, which radical Islamists virulently condemn.

As against the Islamist trend, in more recent years, independent Arab intellectuals have tried to treat Kawakibi in a more scientific way and stress his progressive ideas on education, democracy, and humanism. One of the pioneering efforts in this direction was the 1980s research by the Lebanese scholar Jan Daya, the first to locate surviving copies of *al-Shahba* and *al-I'tidal*. Daya's book on Kawakibi's journalism concludes with "An Answer to Sylvia Haim," in which, in the spirit of Edward Said's *Orientalism*, he refutes not only her claim of plagiarism, but also her underlying presumption that Arab intellectuals must have borrowed their ideas from the West.

The centenary of Abd al-Rahman al-Kawakibi's death in 2002 gave the Arab intellectuals further opportunity to self-critically reflect on their political and social mission. At conferences held on this occasion in Aleppo, co-organized by his great grandson Salam al-Kawakibi, and in Amman in the presence of Sa'd Zaghlul al-Kawakibi, concern was expressed at the fate of the cumulative endeavors of successive generations of Arab intellectuals for the sake of their nation's revival and progress. The organizers of the Aleppo conference lamented the absence of freedom of speech, thought, and research throughout the Arab world, as well as the isolation of the intellectuals from government, educational institutions, and the media, and their lack of broad social support of the citizenry, as the major causes for the ineffectiveness of their call. The situation they described was not much different from the realities in Kawakibi's day of the *nahda* under the despotic rule of Sultan Abdulhamid II. The blame was to be laid partly on the intellectuals themselves, who preferred to address each other in their narrow circles and had no respect for or trust in the masses. But this was felt to be excusable in view of the persistence of tyranny in practically all the Arab countries and the concomitant rise of an oppositional Islamic radicalism. The intellectuals' predicament had been illustrated two years earlier by the tribulations of the Kawakibi Forum for Democratic Dialogue, launched during the "Damascus Spring" promised by Bashar al-Assad on his ascent to power in 2000. The Forum stimulated open debate on matters of state and society among growing numbers of writers across Syria, but a government crackdown in 2003 sent most of them to jail.

Outside Syria, there have been attempts since then to give more consideration to Kawakibi's concrete proposals for reform in the Arab and Islamic realms alike. A large meeting that brought together forty civil society groups from the Middle East and North Africa (MENA) in September 2004 in Beirut evoked Kawakibi's denunciation of despotism to prescribe "a program of structural reform," stretching from political participation and the rule of law to the guarantee of freedoms, educational reform, and combating corruption. Kawakibi's name likewise looms large as champion of the rights of freedom, accountability, proper education, and religious reform in the series of Arab Human Development Reports issued since 2002 by the United Nations Development Programme (UNDP). And in a declaration published in the *Huffington Post* in the very week I concluded this study, on 17 February 2015, under the title *Muslim Democrats of the World, Unite!*, prominent Muslim leaders Tariq Ramadan, the Swiss-born grandson of Hasan al-Banna and a major ideologue of Euro-Islam, Anwar Ibrahim, the liberal former Vice-President of Malaysia, and others call, in the face of the "barbarous murderers" of ISIS and Boko Haram, for a "relaunch [of] the reformist work of ijtihad undertaken by Muhammad Abduh, Abd al-Rahman al-Kawakibi and Muhammad Iqbal at the turn of the 20th century" and "constantly advocate moderation and a reformist approach to issues of religious education, governance, the rule of law, freedom of expression and the protection of fundamental liberties." Kawakibi would certainly have agreed with these declarations and programs, but would have felt frustrated knowing that the same issues that so concerned him in the later part of the nineteenth century still head the agenda of his Arab-Islamic intellectual heirs after the turn of the twenty-first century.

A FINAL ASSESSMENT

This study of Abd al-Rahman al-Kawakibi has shown him to be one of the most original thinkers of the Modernist Salafi and Arab renaissance trends of the late nineteenth century, and one of the major sources of Islamic reform and Arab nationalism in the twentieth and into the twenty-first century. Of course, every thinker is influenced by the ideas current in his time and place. Kawakibi's circumstances, however, which forced him to conceal his thought for most of his mature life, make it particularly difficult to identify the exact provenance of each of his specific ideas. In the political field, which was his earliest concern, it is abundantly clear that, as a native of Aleppo, Kawakibi was widely exposed to the ideas of the Young Ottomans, and toward the end of his life apparently to those of the Young Turks as well, much more than his colleagues farther south in Syria or in Egypt. Hence his strong anti-autocratic stance and his espousal of the patriotic, liberalist, democratic, and socialist causes.

In the religious field, which was added in due course, Kawakibi subscribed to many of the ideas prevalent among the reformist intellectual circles of the period. Like them, he called for a return to the example of the forefathers, adherence to the scriptures, the use of reason, and amendment of the scholarly and especially Sufi traditions. Still, as perceptively observed many years ago by Hourani, such ideas were "in the air" among groups of reformers in the more advanced Muslim countries, so it would be a simplification to explain them in terms of the influence of Afghani and Abduh. Indeed, Kawakibi's originality lies in his particular politico-religious synthesis founded on the secular idea of separation of religion from state, in his performative style of public deliberation and scientific research, and in his practical suggestions to establish an association for Muslim edification and to restore the Caliphate to the Arabs.

It is no less difficult to trace Kawakibi's influence on subsequent generations of Islamic reformers, Arab nationalists, and liberal intellectuals at large. As we have seen, in a way, all trends have acknowledged their indebtedness to the great precursor. It is extremely doubtful, however, that Kawakibi himself would have favored the authoritarian regimes of Abdul Nasser and the Ba'th, or the violent methods of al-Qaeda and the ISIS Caliphate. He also certainly would have shared the liberal intellectuals' self-criticism of their impotence in the face of these destructive forces. A study of the impact of specific ideas of Kawakibi on subsequent thinkers is yet to be undertaken. Such an enterprise would involve, in the first place, a deconstruction of the Afghani–Abduh–Rida line and the attribution of the roots of some major ideas of the later Rida – the notion of moderate Salafism, the propagation of Islam (*da'wa*), and the Islamic state – to Kawakibi. It would then trace the adoption of certain of these ideas by Rida's various successors: the contemporary conservative Salafis, the progressive Modernists, and the Muslim Brotherhood activists. Such a study would show that – the focus on some of Kawakibi's ideas notwithstanding – the failure to embrace his balanced spiritual and practical synthesis in its entirety in a sense epitomizes the past and present upheavals of the modern Middle East. It might also light the way to some brighter future.

BIBLIOGRAPHY

Archives

Les archives diplomatiques du ministère des affaires étrangères, Paris and Nantes

The British National Archives, London

Başbakanlık Osmanlı Arşivleri, Istanbul

Journals

al-Shahba'

al-I'tidal

al-Manar

Books and articles

Abu Hamdan, Samir. *'Abd al-Rahman al-Kawakibi wa-falsafat al-istibdad* (Beirut: al-Shariqa al-'alamiyya li'l-kitab, 1992).

Abu-Manneh, Butrus. "Sultan Abdulhamid II and Shaikh Abulhuda al-Sayyadi," *Middle Eastern Studies* 15 (1979), 131–53.

Adunis and Khalida Sa'id. *Diwan al-nahda: al-Kawakibi* (Beirut: Dar al-ilm li'l-mala'in, 1982).

Amara, Muhammad. *'Abd al-Rahman al-Kawakibi – shahid al-huriyya wa-mujaddid al-Islam* (Cairo: Dar al-shuruq, 2007).

Amin, Ahmad. *Zua'ma al-islah fi al-'asr al-hadith* (Cairo: Maktabat al-nahda al-misriyya, 1949).

Amin, 'Uthman. *Ru'ad al-wa'y al-insani fi al-sharq al-islami* (Cairo: al-Hai'a al-misriyya al-'amma li'l-kitab, 2001).

Antonius, George. *The Arab Awakening* (Beirut: Khayat's, 1938).

al-'Aqqad, 'Abbas Mahmud. *'Abd al-Rahman al-Kawakibi* (Cairo: Majlis al-'la li-ria'yat al-funun wa-al-adab wa-al-'ulum al-ijtima'iyya, 1959).

Atiyeh, G. N. "Humanism and Secularism in the Modern Arab Heritage: The Ideas of Kawakibi and Zurayk," in G. N. Atiyeh and Ibrahim M. Oweiss (eds.), *Arab Civilization: Challenges and Responses: Studies in honor of Constantine K. Zurayk* (Albany: State University of New York Press, 1988), 42–59.

al-'Awadi, Zaki 'Ali (ed.). *Harakat al-islah fi al-asr al-hadith: 'Abd al-Rahman al-Kawakibi namudhajan* (Amman: Dar al-Razi, 2004).

'Ayntabi, Muhammad Fu'ad. *Halab fi mi'a 'am, 1850–1950* (Aleppo: Jam'iyyat Halab, Ma'had al-turath al-'ilmi al-'arabi, 1993).

Barqawi, Ahmad Nasim. *Muhawala fi qira'at 'asr al-nahda, al-islah al-dini, al-nuzha al-qawmiyya* (Damascus: al-Ahali, 1999).

Barut, Jamil. *Harakat al-tanwir al-'arabiyya fi al-qarn al-tasi' 'ashar* (Damascus: n.p., 1994).

Burj, Muhammad 'Abd al-Rahman. *'Abd al-Rahman al-Kawakibi* (Cairo: al-Hai'a al-misriyya al-'amma li'l-kitab, 1972).

al-Dabbagh, 'Aisha. *al-Haraka al-fikriyya fi Halab fi al-nisf al-thani min al-qarn al-tasi' 'ashar* (Beirut: Dar al-fikr, 1972).

al-Dahhan, Sami. *'Abd al-Rahman al-Kawakibi* (Cairo: Dar al-ma'arif, 1958).

— *Qudama' wa-mu'asirun* (Cairo: Dar al-ma'arif, 1961).

Dawish, Adeed. *Arab Nationalism in the Twentieth Century: From Triumph to Despair* (Princeton: Princeton University Press, 2003).

Dawn, C. Ernest. "The Origins of Arab Nationalism," in Rashid Khalidi, Lisa Anderson, Muhammad Muslih, and Reeva S. Simon (eds.), *The Origins of Arab Nationalism* (New York: Columbia University Press, 1991), 3–30.

Daya, Jan. *al-Imam al-Kawakibi: Fasl al-din an al-dawla* (London: Dar Sourakia, 1988).

— *Sihafat al-Kawakibi* (Beirut: Mu'assasat fikr li'l-abhath wa'l-nashr, 1984).

al-Dhawadi, Zuhayr. *al-Khuruj min nasq al-dawla al-diniyya* (Beirut: Mua'sassat al-intishar al-'arabi, 2010).

Eich, Thomas. *Abu al-Huda as-Sayyadi: Eine Studie zur Instrumentaliserung sufische Netzwerke und genealogischer Kontroversen in spätosmanischen Reich* (Berlin: Klaus Schwarz Verlag, 2003).

Eldem, Edhem, Daniel Goffman and Bruce Masters. *The Ottoman City between East and West: Aleppo, Izmir, and Istanbul* (Cambridge: Cambridge University Press, 1999).

Farah, Caesar. E. "Nationalist Concerns for Syria: The Case of Farah Antun, Mayy Ziadah, and al-Kawakibi," in Adel Beshara (ed.), *The Origins of Syrian Nationhood: Histories, Pioneers and Identity* (New York and London: Routledge, 2011), 210–22.

Funatsu, Ryuichi. "Al-Kawakibi's Thesis and its Echoes in the Arab World Today," *Harvard Middle Eastern and Islamic Review* 7 (2006), 1–40.

Gaulmier, Jean. "Note sur l'état présent de l'enseignement traditional à Alep," *Bulletin d'études orientales* 9 (1942–3), 13–27.

al-Ghazzi, Kamil. *Nahr al-dhahab fi tarikh Halab* (3 vols., Aleppo: al-Matba'a al-marwaniyya, 1923–26).

— "Abd al-Rahman al-Kawakibi: Tarikh ma ahmalahu al-tarikh min siratihi," *al-Hadith* 3 (1929), 405–20, 445–50.

Gonnella, Julia. "As-Sayyid Abu al-Huda al-Sayyadi in Aleppo," in Jens Hanssen, Thomas Philipp and Stefan Weber (eds.), *The Empire in the City: Arab Provincial Capitals in the Late Ottoman Empire* (Beirut: Ergon Verlag, 2002), 297–307.

Haim, Sylvia G. "Alfieri and al-Kawakibi," *Oriente Moderno* 34 (1954), 132–43.

— "Blunt and al-Kawakibi," *Oriente Moderno* 35 (1955), 321–34.

Haq, Mahmudul. "'Abd al-Rahman al-Kawakibi (1854–1902): A Study in Transition from Islamic Revivalism to Arab Nationalism," *Bulletin of the Institute of Islamic Studies* 8–9 (1965), 49–63.

al-Himsi, Qustaqi. *Udaba' Halab dhawu al-athar fi al-qarn al-tasi' 'ashar* (Aleppo: al-Matba'a al-maruniyya, 1925).

Hourani, Albert. *Arabic Thought in the Liberal Age, 1789–1939* (London: Oxford University Press, 1962).

Husry, Khaldun S. *Three Reformers: A Study in Modern Arab Political Thought* (Beirut: Khayat's, 1966).

Jamsheer, Hassan. "Arab-Islamic Revival (Nahda) in 'Abd al-Rahman al-Kawakibi's Socio-Political Thought," *Rocznik Orientalistyczny* 55 (2003), 91–108.

Jankowski, James and Israel Gershoni (eds.). *Rethinking Arab Nationalism in the Arab World* (New York: Columbia University Press, 1997).

Juha, Farid. *al-Hayah al-fikriyya fi Halab fi al-qarn al-tasi' 'ashar* (Damascus: al-Ahali, 1988).

Kabbara, Nazih. *'Abd al-Rahman al-Kawakibi: hayatuhu wa-'asruhu wa-ara'uhu* (Tripoli: Jarrus Bras, 1994).

Katura, Jurj. *Tabai' al-Kawakibi fi Taba'i' al-istibdad* (Beirut: al-Mu'assasa al-jami'iyya, 1987).

al-Kawakibi, 'Abd al-Rahman. *Taba'i' al-istibdad wa-masari' al-isti'bad* (1st ed. Cairo: n.p., 1900; 2nd ed. Aleppo: al-Matba'a al-'asriyya, 1957).

— *Umm al-Qura* (1st ed. Port Said: al-Sayyid al-Furati, 1900; 2nd ed. Aleppo: Matba'at al-ma'arif, 1959).

al-Kawakibi, As'ad. "Abd al-Rahman al-Kawakibi," *al-Hadith* 26 (1952), 542–54.

al-Kawakibi, Sa'd Zaghlul. *'Abd al-Rahman al-Kawakibi: al-sira al-dhatiyya* (Beirut: Bisan li'l-nashr wa'l-tawzi', 1998).

Kawakibi, Salam. "Un réformateur et la science," *Revue des Mondes Musulmans et de la Méditerranée* 101–2 (2013), 69–82.

al-Kayyali, Sami. *al-Adab al-'Arabi al-mu'asir fi Suriya, 1850–1950* (Cairo: Dar al-ma'arif, 1959).

Kedourie, Elie. "The Politics of Political Literature: Kawakibi, Azoury and Jung," in his *Arabic Political Memoirs* (London: Frank Cass, 1974), 107–23.

Khalafallah, Muhammad Ahmad. *al-Kawakibi – hayatuhu wa-arauhu* (Cairo: Maktabat al-'Arab, 1950).

Khoury, Philip S. *Urban Notables and Arab Nationalism: The Politics of Damascus 1860–1920* (Cambridge: Cambridge University Press, 1983).

Kramer, Martin. *Islam Assembled: The Advent of Muslim Congresses* (New York: Columbia University Press, 1986).

Kurd 'Ali, Muhammad. *Al-Mudhakkirat* (4 vols., Damascus: Matba'at al-Turki, 1948–51).

Lauzière, Henri. "The Evolution of the Salafiyya in the Twentieth Century through the Life and Thought of Taqi al-Din al-Hilali." Ph.D. Dissertation, Georgetown University, 2008.

al-Maladhi, Suhayl. *al-Tiba'a wa'l-sihafa fi Halab* (Damascus: Dar ya'rib, 1996).

Ma'oz, Moshe. *Ottoman Reform in Syria and Palestine, 1840–1861* (Oxford: Oxford University Press, 1968).

Marcus, Abraham. *The Middle East on the Eve of Modernity: Aleppo in the Eighteenth Century* (New York: Columbia University Press, 1989).

Masters, Bruce. "Power and Society in Aleppo in the 18th and 19th Centuries," in *Alep et la Syrie du Nord, Revue du monde musulman et de la Méditerranée* 62 (1991–4), 151–8.

— "The 1850 Events in Aleppo: An Aftershock of Syria's Incorporation into the Capitalist World System," *International Journal of Middle East Studies* 22 (1990), 3–20.

al-Najjar, Ibrahim Salim. "Abd al-Rahman al-Kawakibi (min dhikriy-yat al-madi)," *al-Hadith* 14 (1940), 3–7.

Nuseibeh, Hazem Zaki. *The Ideas of Arab Nationalism* (Ithaca, NY: Cornell University Press, 1956).

Pellittery, Antonino. *'Abd al-Rahman al-Kawakibi (1853/4–1902): Nuovi Materiali Bio-Bibliografici* (Roma: Istituto per l'Oriente, 1998).

— "Etat moderne, société et reform: la vision d'al-Kawakibi (mort 1902) d'après al-Šahba et l'I'tidal," in M. Petricioli and A. Tonini (eds.), *Identità e appartenenze in Medio Oriente* (Florence: University of Florence, 1998), 29–38.

Qala'aji, Qadri. *'Abd al-Rahman al-Kawakibi* (Beirut: Dar al-sharq al-jadid, 1963).

Rabbat, Gabriel. "Notice sur la vie et les travaux du Sheikh Kamel el-Ghazzy," *Revue Archeologique Syrienne* 3 (1933), 1–3.

Rahme, Joseph G. "'Abd al-Rahman al-Kawakibi's Reformist

Ideology, Arab Pan-Islamism, and the Internal Other," *Journal of Islamic Studies* 10 (1999), 159–77.

Raymond André. "Alep à l'époque ottomane (XVIe–XIXe siècles)," *Revue du monde musulman et de la Méditerranée* 62 (1991), 93–109.

Raz, R. "Interpretations of Kawakibi's Thought, 1950–1980s," *Middle Eastern Studies* 32 (1996), 179–90.

Rida, Muhammad Rashid. "Musab 'azim bi-wafat 'alim hakim," *al-Manar* 5 (1902), 237–40, 276–80.

Roded, Ruth. "Tradition and Change in Syria during the Last Decades of Ottoman Rule: The Urban Elite of Damascus, Aleppo, Homs and Hama, 1876–1914." Ph.D. Dissertation, University of Denver, 1984.

Rogan, Eugene. "Instant Communication: The Impact of the Telegraph in Ottoman Syria," in Thomas Philipp and Brigit Schaebler (eds.), *The Syrian Land: Process of Integration and Fragmentation, Bilad al-Sham from the 18th to the 20th Century* (Stuttgart: F. Steiner, 1998), 113–28.

al-Sahmarani, As'ad. *al-Istibdad wa'l-isti'mar wa-turuq muwajahatiha 'inda al-Kawakibi wa'l-Ibrahimi* (Beirut: Dar al-nafa'is, 1984).

Samra, Mahmud. "Islamic Modernism: Self-Criticism and Revivalism in Syrian Muslim Thinkers," in E. H. Waugh, Baha Abu-Laban and R. B. Qureshi (eds.), *The Muslim Community in North America* (Edmonton: University of Alberta Press, 1983), 34–49.

al-Sharif, Mahir and Salam al-Kawakibi (eds.). *Tayyar al-islah al-dini wa-masa'iruhu fi al-mujtama'at al-'arabiyya: awraq al-'amal al-muqaddama fi al-nadwa al-mun'aqada bi-munasabat al-dhikra al-mia'iyya li'l-rahil al-imam 'Abd al-Rahman al-Kawakibi* (Damascus: French Institute of Arab Studies, 2002).

Shaykhu, Luis. *Tarikh al-adab al-'arabiyya fi al-rub' al-awwal min al-qarn al-'ishrin* (Beirut: al-Matba'a al-Kathulikiyya, 1926).

Sluglett, Peter. "Aspects of Economy and Society in the Syrian Provinces: Aleppo in Transition, 1880–1925," in Leila Tarazi Fawaz and C. A. Bayly (eds.), *Modernity and Culture from the Mediterranean to the Indian Ocean* (New York: Columbia University Press, 2001), 144–57.

al-Tabbakh, Muhammad Raghib. *I'lam al-nubala' bi-tarikh Halab al-Shahba'* (2nd ed., 7 vols., Aleppo: Dar al-qalam al-arabi, 1988).

al-Tahhan, Muhammad Jamal. *'Awdat al-Kawakibi: Hayat al-mufakkir al-tha'ir wa-a'maluhu* (Aleppo: n.p., 2006).

— *al-Istibdad wa-bada'iluhu fi fikr al-Kawakibi* (Damascus: Ittihad al-kitab al-'arabi, 1992).

— *al-Ru'ya al-islahiyya li'l-mufakkir al-nahdawi 'Abd al-Rahman al-Kawakibi: Qira'a mu'asira* (Damascus: Ittihad al-kuttab al-'arab, 2007).

Tapiero, Norbert. *Les idées réformistes d'al-Kawakibi, 1265–1320 – 1849–1902. Contribution á l'étude de l'Islam moderne* (Paris: Les Editions Arabes, 1956).

Tarazi, Filib di. *Ta'rikh al-sahafa al-'arabiyya* (Beirut: American Press, 1933).

Tauber, Eliezer. "Three Approaches, One Idea: Religion and State in the Thought of 'Abd al-Rahman al-Kawakibi, Najib Azuri and Rashid Rida," *British Journal of Middle Eastern Studies* 21 (1994), 190–8.

Turroni, Giuliana. "'Abd al-Rahman al-Kawakibi: una variante laica del riformismo Islamico ottocentesco," in Gian Mario Bravo (ed.), *La Democrazia Tra Liberta e Tirannide della Maggioranza Nell'Ottocento* (Florence: Leo S. Olschki Editore, MMIV), 283–342.

Watenpaugh, Keith. *Being Modern in the Middle East: Revolution, Nationalism, Colonialism, and the Arab Middle Class* (Princeton: Princeton University Press, 2006).

Weismann, Itzchak. "The Hidden Hand: The Khalidiyya and the Orthodox–Fundamentalist Nexus in Aleppo," *Journal of the History of Sufism* 5 (2007), 41–59.

Wirth, Eugen. "Alep dans la première moitié du XIXe siècle: un exemple de stabilité et de dynamique dans l'économie ottoman tardive," *Revue du monde musulman et de la Méditerranée* 62 (1991), 133–49.

al-Zaidi, Muhammad Rajab. *Muslihun tha'irun: 'Abd al-Rahman al-Kawakibi, Jamal al-Din al-Afghani, Muhammad 'Abduh* (Benghazi: Dar al-kitab al-Libi, 1972).

Zaydan, Jurji. *Tarajim mashahir al-Sharq fi al-qarn al-tasi' 'ashar* (2 vols., Cairo: Dar al-hilal, 1910–11).

Zeine, Zeine N. *The Emergence of Arab Nationalism* (Beirut: Khayat's 1966).

al-Zirikli, Khayr al-Din. *A'lam – qamus tarajim li-ashhar al-rijal wa'l-nisa' min al-'Arab wa'l-musta'aribin wa'l-mustashriqin* (10 vols., Cairo: n.p., 1954–9).

Websites

al-Jazira.net. Abd al-Rahman al-Kawakibi
http://www.aljazeera.net/knowledgegate/books/2007/8/13/%d8%b9%d8%a8%d8%af-%d8%a7%d9%84%d8%b1%d8%ad%d9%85%d9%86-%d8%a7%d9%84%d9%83%d9%88%d8%a7%d9%83%d8%a8%d9%8a

Kashf al-masuni al-maqbur Abd al-Rahman al-Kawakibi
http://www.youtube.com/watch?v=HwNJoS_zOgA

Hafidat al-Kawakibi fi awal hiwar li'l-Ahram: jiddi 'asha munaddilan wa-qutila ghadran wa-dafa'a thaman nidalihi maratayn
http://www.ahram.org.eg/News/815/83/209063/%D8%A7%D9%84%D8%AD%D9%88%D8%A7%D8%B1/%D8%AD%D9%81%D9%8A%D8%AF%D8%A9-%D8%A7%D9%84%D9%83%D9%88%D8%A7%D9%83%D8%A8%D9%8A-%D9%81%D9%8A-%D8%A3%D9%88%D9%84-%D8%AD%D9%88%D8%A7%D8%B1-%D9%84%D9%84%D8%A3%D9%87%D8%B1%D8%A7%D9%85%E2%80%8F%E2%80%8F%D8%AC%D8%AF%D9%8A-%D8%B9%D8%A7%D8%B4-%D9%85%D9%86%D8%A7%D8%B6%D9%84%D8%A7.aspx

Qisas li'l-atfal – Abu al-du'afa': Abd al-Rahman al-Kawakibi
http://www.nashiri.net/stories/children-stories/1146-ez--v15-1146.html

Muslim Democrats of the World, Unite!
http://www.huffingtonpost.com/felix-marquardt/muslim-democrats-unite_b_6648898.html

INDEX